Pitt Series in Policy and Institutional Studies

Fragile Democracies

The Legacies of Authoritarian Rule

Gretchen Casper

UNIVERSITY OF PITTSBURGH PRESS
PITTSBURGH AND LONDON

Published by the University of Pittsburgh Press, Pittsburgh, Pa. 15260

Copyright © 1995, University of Pittsburgh Press
All rights reserved
Eurospan, London
Manufactured in the United States of America
Printed on acid-free paper

Library of Congress Cataloging-in-Publication Data

Casper, Gretchen, 1958–
    Fragile democracies : legacies of authoritarian rule /
Gretchen Casper.
        p.   cm. — (Pitt series in policy and institutional studies)
    Includes bibliographical references (p.   ).
    ISBN 0-8229-3857-X (acid-free paper). — ISBN 0-8229-5540-7 (pbk.
: acid-free paper)
    1. Philippines—Politics and government—1973–1986.
2. Philippines—Politics and government—1986–   3. Authoritarianism—
Philippines.   4. Democracy—Philippines.   5. Civil-military
relations—Philippines.   6. Religion and politics—Philippines.
I. Title.   II. Series.
JQ1416.C37   1994
320.9599'09'048—dc20   94-39782
                                                                CIP

A CIP catalogue record for this book is available from the British Library.

Contents

Acknowledgments

The idea for comparing the church and the military in the Philippines and Latin America began while I was an instructor at Grinnell College. Although I would never recommend that someone finish writing their dissertation, teach at a prestigious liberal arts college, and start on a new project all in the same year, I must say that my experience was eased and enriched by the students and faculty at Grinnell College. My colleagues in political science—Robert Grey, Bud Strauber, Wayne Moyer, and Mike Hawthorne—encouraged my research and presented me with a very high standard of collegiality and teaching.

My interest in religion and politics was sparked by a class I took from Dan Levine during my first year as a graduate student at Michigan. He was also the first person who encouraged me to compare the Philippines with Latin America, thereby ignoring disciplinary barriers and opting instead for theoretical richness. Deborah Norden, the late Charles Gillespie, David Pion-Berlin, and Wendy Hunter continued to hold this cross-regional door open for me, for which I am thankful. When the manuscript was in its initial draft, Melanie Manion, David Pion-Berlin, and Bob Youngblood read it and offered their advice. I would also like to thank Bert Rockman for giving the manuscript a home in his series.

In the Philippines, the Institute for Philippine Culture gave me office space and credentials as a visiting research associate. My work was aided by help from Cora Bolong, Fr. John Carroll, S.J., Fr. Joaquin G. Bernas, S.J., Dr. Jose P. Abueva, Col. (ret.) Salvador Z. Ramiro and Fredezvinda Ty Ramiro, Sr. Teresa Joseph

Patrick of Jesus and Mary OCD, Atty. Luis Mauricio, Atty. Luz M. Villamor, Atty. Hermengilda Abejo, the late Atty. Beatriz J. Gonzales, Atty. Florencio B. Orendain, Jr., Dr. Romana De Los Reyes, Dr. Virginia Miralao, Frankie Jose, and Nora Reyes. This project would not have been possible without the cooperation and trust of the informants, who not only talked with me but also suggested others with whom I should meet.

I would like to thank my colleagues at Texas A & M University, especially Frank Baumgartner, Jon Bond, George Edwards, Bryan Jones, Alex Mintz, Jonathan Nagler, and Misha Taylor, for offering early support for half-baked ideas. Frank Baumgartner and Misha Taylor deserve special recognition for reading the entire manuscript and remaining enthusiastic. I received help on data collection, coding, final manuscript preparation, and general problem solving from Marcia Bastian, Peter Ferguson, Doug Gilkey, Karlina Greenfield, Uk Heo, Carolyn Ismert, Ranjana Mehra, Kevin O'Neill, Betty Rosser, Randy Stevenson, Hans Stockton, and Leticia Villareal.

This book received considerable financial support from Texas A & M University—from the Department of Political Science, the College of Liberal Arts, the University Honors Program, the Military Studies Institute, the Office of International Coordination, and the Institute for Pacific-Asia. I was awarded a Research Opportunities for Women grant (SES-8910232) from the National Science Foundation for 1989. Finally, the University of Michigan graciously gave me privileges as a visiting scholar, during the summer of 1990, to conduct archival work in the Hatcher Library.

When conducting work on the Third World, there inevitably comes a time when the researcher runs into a data problem. Needless to say, it is always at the last minute and centers around the linchpin of the argument. I owe a debt of gratitude to Roger Bresnahan, Adolf Gundersen, Michael Martinez, Roberto Vichot, Philip Williams, and especially Hannah Stewart-Gambino for help in tracking down hard-to-find data. If only research on

Third World issues could always be so straightforward as picking up the phone and calling someone somewhere who has the information and is willing to share it with a complete stranger.

For solace and friendship, I thank all those who shared countless meals and tales of frustration at the Chinese restaurant in the converted A&W stand in Newton, Iowa, at the falafel stand on South University in Ann Arbor, Michigan, and at the Thai Taste in Bryan, Texas. It is not an exaggeration to say that generous helpings of camaraderie and Third World cuisine kept this project on track.

Parts of this book, albeit in a different form, were published as articles in *Pilipinas* and *Armed Forces and Society*.

Finally, I would like to thank Len and Linda Casper for teaching Tina and me the importance of living in the Third World in order to understand it, particularly if you are half-Filipina.

List of Abbreviations

AFP	Armed Forces of the Philippines
AID	Agency for International Development
AMRSP	Association of Major Religious Superiors of the Philippines
AVSECOM	Aviation Security Command
BCC	Basic Christian Community (also referred to as BEC or CEB)
BP	Batasang Pambansa–National Assembly
CARP	Comprehensive Agrarian Reform Program
CBCP	Catholic Bishops' Conference of the Philippines
CMLC	Church-Military Liaison Committee
COMELEC	Commission on Elections
ConCom	Constitutional Commission
ConCon	Constitutional Convention
CPP	Communist Party of the Philippines
EDCOR	Economic Development Corps
EDSA	Epifanio De los Santos Avenue
EM	Enlisted Men
FFF	Federation of Free Farmers
FFW	Federation of Free Workers
IBP	interim Batasang Pambansa—interim National Assembly
ICSI	Institute on Church and Social Issues
IMET	International Military Education and Training
INP	Integrated National Police
JUSMAG	Joint United States Military Advisory Group
KBL	Kilusang Bagong Lipunan—New Society Movement

LABAN	Lakas ng Bayan—People Power
MAP	Military Assistance Program
MNLF	Moro National Liberation Front
NAFP	New Armed Forces of the Philippines
NAMFREL	National Movement for Free Elections
NASSA	National Secretariat for Social Action
NISA	National Intelligence and Security Agency
NPA	New People's Army
NPDSP	United Democratic Socialist Party of the Philippines
OICs	Officers-in-Charge
PC	Philippine Constabulary
PMA	Philippine Military Academy
PRODs	Presidential Regional Officers for Development
PSC	Presidential Security Command
RAM	Reform the Armed Forces of the Philippines Movement
UNIDO	United Nationalist Democratic Organization

I

1 The Legacies of Authoritarian Rule

INTRODUCTION

■ In the 1970s, governments in the Philippines and Latin America were led by authoritarian leaders. By the early 1990s, most of these countries had shifted to democracy. In the mid 1990s, observers are concluding that redemocratization is the future, returning to the optimistic analyses of the 1950s and 1960s, when modernization theory held that democracy would spread throughout the Third World. Just as scholars were surprised by the imposition of authoritarian regimes in many countries in the 1970s, I argue in this book that a focus on redemocratization in the 1990s understates the problems inherent in the transition from authoritarianism.

This book discusses the legacies of authoritarianism and how difficult it is for well-meaning new leaders to ensure that the new democracy will flourish. Even in countries with a strong democratic tradition, such as the Philippines, evidence presented here demonstrates that redemocratization remains problematic at best. Authoritarian regimes leave an imprint on society long after their leaders have been overthrown because they systematically seek to alter the traditional roles of important social institutions. By forcing groups such as the church and the military to play an active political role, the authoritarian regime inadvertently guarantees that these and other institutions will continue to intervene

3

in politics. Thus, the legacies of authoritarian rule are fragile democracies.

This book builds a model to explain why social institutions
such as the church and the military remain in the political arena
after redemocratization. Under authoritarianism, these institutions are pulled into an active political stance, either in support
of the regime (in the case of the military), or in opposition to it
(as with the church). This change in the traditional role of the
institution creates internal strains, since it creates subgroups
within the institution with competing and incompatible goals.
Some seek to return to the traditional role as quickly as possible
after the demise of the authoritarian leader, but others hope to
remain active in the political realm. These divisions are compounded by the condition of other traditional social actors, such
as labor unions, political parties, and interest groups, often the
targets of neutralization or suppression by the authoritarian
leader. In other words, authoritarian leaders transform or destroy
the social institutions on which a successful democracy depends.
Simply replacing the leader does not redress the underlying problems of how interests will be articulated under the new leadership, however well meaning it may be.

Evidence for the model is based on extensive examination of
the Marcos and Aquino administrations in the Philippines and
on a review of the secondary literature on several Latin American
countries. During fieldwork in Manila in 1988, I conducted
sixty-seven interviews with a broad range of officials in the church
and in the military and with journalists, academics, and other
knowledgeable observers. The people interviewed include many
of those involved in the movement to rid the country of Marcos,
as well as those involved in subsequent coup attempts against
Aquino.

Individuals in the church or the military were approached to
suggest names for informants. After the interview was completed,
each informant was then asked to suggest other people to be
interviewed. The informants who were chosen to be interviewed

differed in terms of intensity of support or opposition to the Marcos regime. They also differed in the types of political activities that they engaged in and that they believed their institutions should follow.

Each informant was asked a structured, open-ended interview schedule that focused on five basic topics, with follow-up questions. (The interview schedule is in the appendix.) The questions captured when and how the informants' institutions changed their activities to become more political, the role the institutions played in the 1986 regime change, and the enduring effects of such activities and roles on the institutions. The interviews ranged approximately from thirty minutes to several hours. The interviews were not taped, to put the informants at ease. Archival work was then carried out to corroborate and complete the information from the interviews.

While the interviews provide a great deal of context, the analysis is also based on extensive documentation from primary and secondary sources in the Philippines and the United States. Information from secondary sources on a number of Latin American cases points to the generalizability of the model developed in the Philippine context.

THE LEGACIES OF AUTHORITARIAN RULE

The legacies of authoritarian rule are fragile democracies. In the short term, the regime changes the rules of the game to install itself and maintain its control over the political arena. For example, a regime will suspend the constitution by declaring martial law. The regime will either close down political institutions and groups that traditionally channel mass participation—such as legislatures, political parties, and labor unions—or will severely narrow their scope of activity. Such structural changes reduce the number of power centers independent of the regime and also increase the regime's ability to coordinate mass participation.

Both of these developments increase the regime's power in and control over society.

While a regime may introduce structural changes to institutionalize itself, the chances of success are actually low because of the enormity of the task: the regime must be able to monopolize avenues to power, amass capital, gain societal support, and convince elites to cooperate (Stepan 1978, 292). Most scholarship on authoritarianism has acknowledged this dilemma, focusing on the short-term problems that such regimes face to remain in power. Whether the causes of instability are the erosion of the regime's basis for legitimacy because of poor economic performance (Epstein 1984), the defection of key members of the regime's support coalition (Hirschman 1970; Linz 1973; O'Donnell 1978; Cardoso 1986), conflict within the ruling bloc itself, or the emergence of a credible alternative leader (Przeworski 1986), all of these scholars agree that authoritarianism is an unstable form of government. Thus, the short-term effect of authoritarianism is regime collapse.

The wave of regime collapse in the eighties and nineties in the Third World, particularly in Latin America, has focused scholarship on redemocratization (Huntington 1984; Gastil 1985; Remmer 1985; Viola and Mainwaring 1985; O'Donnell, Schmitter, and Whitehead 1986; Overholt 1986; Stepan 1986; Lopez and Stohl 1987; Mainwaring 1988; Rochon and Mitchell 1989; Diamond, Linz, and Lipset 1989; McClintock 1989; Di Palma 1990; Huntington 1991; Przeworski 1991; Remmer 1991; Higley and Gunther 1992). Many scholars view this transition out of authoritarianism toward democracy in an optimistic light. Indeed, citizens' euphoria over such regime collapse is matched by scholars' predictions that democratic consolidation will succeed. For example, Seligson argues that the recent trend of democratization in Latin America will be more robust than that in the 1950s, because the military regimes' disastrous performances delegitimized them as credible governments and because the rise of socioeconomic levels in the region is above a minimum threshold for democracy (Seligson 1987, 9–10).

However, political instability does not end with the collapse of authoritarianism and the introduction of or return to democracy. The experience of authoritarianism also threatens the postauthoritarian government because institutions and groups cannot revert back to their preauthoritarian behavior or structures. By implementing authoritarianism, not only does the regime constrain old rules and institutions, it also creates new ones. New rules are devised, either formally, through the drafting of new constitutions or the release of executive orders, or informally, through negotiations within the regime's support coalition. New institutions are created, such as a ruling junta and Congress, and new political actors are positioned in power, such as the military. Thus, the legacy of authoritarianism is a radical restructuring of the political arena.

Just as the installation of authoritarianism does not ensure its institutionalization, neither does the installation of democracy ensure its success. There are several reasons to be pessimistic, rather than optimistic, over the chances of these new governments surviving. Rules of the game (Rustow 1970; Levine 1978) may never be agreed upon by competing elites; thus, any unification of the opposition to oust an authoritarian regime will quickly refragment. The original impetus for the transition— from above rather than below—can also hinder consolidation. While it is easier to install a government from above, it is less likely that that government will introduce reform; on the other hand, democracies installed from below are less likely to be stable (Alves 1988; Karl 1990).

A NEW MODEL

This book argues that the best way to understand the legacy of authoritarianism is to study social institutions, such as the church and the military. First, these institutions organize both mass and elite actors, thus affecting the values and behavior of a wide cross-section of society. Second, they exist independent of the regime. They are already in place as the authoritarian regime is installed and are critical to the success of the democratization process after the regime collapses. Third, because they are independent, they are seen by the regime as potential rivals. Therefore, the regime tries either to gain their loyalty or to suppress their activity.

This book, then, takes an institutional approach to study authoritarianism. Unlike Huntington, who focuses on the interaction between political institutions and the mass public to see if the former can develop quickly enough to absorb the latter (1968), this book focuses on the interaction between social institutions and the regime. It argues that institutions develop new beliefs and slowly change their behavior vis-à-vis the regime in order to reflect their changing beliefs. Once major social institutions change in such a way, it is unlikely that they will revert to their previous behavior. (For similar arguments in other contexts, see March and Olsen 1984 and Krasner 1984.)

This book follows the parallel developments within two social institutions—the church and the military—as their ideologies change. It also looks at the interaction between these institutions and the regime, as the latter tries to influence their roles and behavior. It studies the institutions across time, from before authoritarianism is installed through their experiences under the regime and into the democratization process.

The experience of authoritarianism changes social institutions. (See figure 1.) In the short term, this change leads to the institutions defecting from the authoritarian regime's support coalition, causing its collapse. In the long run, the experiences that the institutions undergo can threaten democratic consolidation, as the institutions are trying to simultaneously reunify their membership and reidentify their roles in society.

The institutions themselves are in a dynamic state. Across time, they change their roles as new ideologies emerge within

FIGURE 1
The Legacy of Authoritarianism

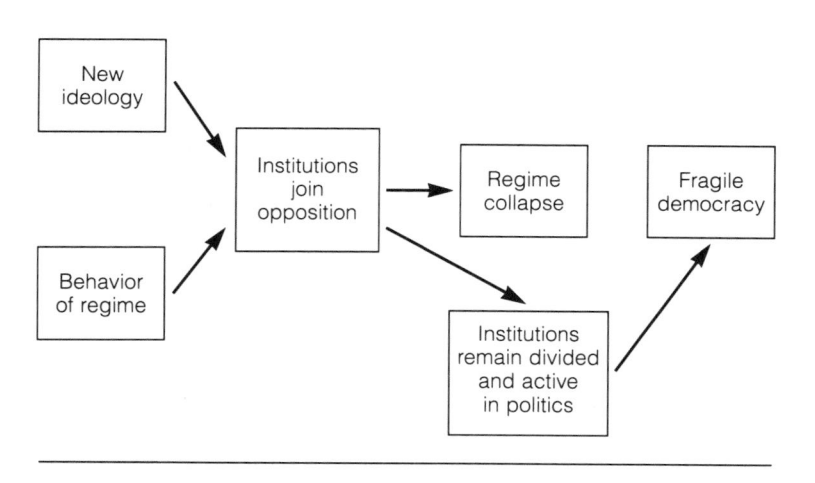

them that introduce new goals and target new clients. Further-more, this change fragments the institutions, as groups within each institution support different roles and ideologies. Thus, in-stitutions will be experiencing internal stress.

This internal dynamic is compounded by the regime's behav-ior toward them. By instituting martial law, the regime itself influences the institutions' roles. Since the regime needs to main-tain its support coalition to remain in power, it institutes a series of carrots and sticks to keep their loyalty. The regime's behavior increases strains within the institutions, as competing goals are formed: one to support the regime, and another to remain loyal to the institutions' traditional roles.

Opposition arises, then, as regime behavior harms institutional interests. For example, the church will withdraw support from the regime as the level of human rights violations increases; the military will withdraw as the level of Communist supporters in-creases. As the core interests of the institutions are threatened, their members will increase their opposition to the regime. They will also expand their political activity, moving from speaking out against the regime to acting for its ouster.

As the regime becomes identified as harming rather than helping society, institutions withdraw from the ruling coalition. As original supporters of the authoritarian regime begin to defect, the regime's support base erodes. If the regime realizes that its supporters' interests are shifting, it can protect its coalition by shifting its policies to realign them with their interests. If, on the other hand, the regime ignores the changing interests of its coalition, then its support will erode.

Once regime change occurs, the institutions reassess their political roles. Initially, they may revert to previous low levels of political activity. However, having experienced high levels of activity and having successfully intervened in politics to oust an authoritarian regime, these institutions may reserve for themselves the right to expand their political roles as conditions change.

In the long term, this process of role expansion and regime behavior has serious repercussions for the political stability of the postauthoritarian government. Under authoritarianism, the institutions have become radicalized. When the country tries to return to democracy, these institutions cannot easily revert back to their preauthoritarian roles. This alteration of the institutions leaves their members split as to whether or not the institutions should remain in the political arena or withdraw. Thus, the effect of authoritarianism is the fragmentation of institutions, causing them not only to rise up against the regime but also to try to remain in the political arena even after the democratization process has been introduced.

The following sections discuss this model in depth, with particular application to the two institutions that are analyzed in this book—the Roman Catholic church and the military. The church and the military are selected for this study because they represent diverse groups of the regime's support coalition, both in terms of centrality to the regime and makeup of its membership. The church is a peripheral member of the coalition: it has interests in common with the regime, yet it did not necessarily help establish the regime, nor does it agree with all of the regime's policies. The military, on the other hand, is a core member of the regime's support coalition. The regime depends on the military to protect it and to enforce its policies.

The Emergence of New Ideologies Within Institutions

In theory, the roles of the church and the military historically have been apolitical: the church tends to the souls of its followers and the military implements orders from civilians. However, the actual political roles of the church and the military have been that of regime supporters. Both institutions have used avenues behind the scenes to influence governments.

Under authoritarianism, the church and the military can continue filling this traditional role of government supporter. Both institutions are usually members of the regime's support coalition. Indeed, it is in the regime's interests to keep these institutions as supporters. The regime needs the moral legitimacy and mass support that the church can offer and the social control capabilities of the military.

Although these institutions support the regime, their interests do not remain static. Rather, as the authoritarian regime continues, the institutions undergo role changes. These role changes in turn alter their interests. Thus, the coalition members will be constantly reconsidering their support for the regime.

One stimulus for change comes from within these institutions themselves. As the church's and the military's beliefs change, so too does their rationale for cooperating with the regime. This change is significant for two reasons. First, the new ideology gives the institutions new goals. Second, it targets new clients. Both of these factors cause the church and the military to rethink their support for the authoritarian regime.

For the church, the introduction of a new ideology occurred

in the mid 1960s, with the Second Vatican Council. There, the church shifted its emphasis from salvation to social justice. To the extent that churches in different countries adopted the Vatican II teachings, they also adapted their behavior. Their preference shifted from political stability to human rights. This shift created an opening for more progressive members of the church to move away from supporting the authoritarian regime.

For the military, the new ideology was the introduction of a national security state. Traditionally, the military saw its professionalism as being subservient to civilian leaders. Under the new professionalism, the military developed political and economic skills along with military training. Its focus also shifted from defending the country from external aggressors to ensuring internal security. To the extent that the military in different countries adopted the new professionalism, they also adapted their behavior. Their preference shifted from being under civilians to being equal to them, if not their superiors. This increase in the institution's status was initially supported by the military. However, in the long run, the military's adoption of a new professionalism caused its more traditional members to question their support for the authoritarian regime.

The Impact of Authoritarianism on Social Institutions

The traditional roles of the church and the military are influenced by the introduction of an authoritarian regime and by specific regime behavior. Both of these factors cause the institutions to alter their roles and to oppose the regime. Under authoritarianism, the regime attempts to depoliticize the mass public, through constricting both political institutions and mass participation. (The concept of authoritarianism and its application in the Philippines is developed more fully in chapter 3.) Although the regime is successful in general, it is impossible to completely depoliticize society. Instead, the mass public redirects its participation from traditional political institutions, such as the legislature, to nontraditional ones.

The church is an example of such an institution. When the legislature is closed or controlled, the mass public turns to the church to represent and protect its interests before the regime. People turn to the church because it is a mass-based institution and because of its traditional symbolic role as a moral force in society.

Under authoritarianism, the regime attempts to monopolize power. To justify this action, the regime argues that it needs increased force and control in order to address societal crises. The crises that a regime chooses to justify its switch to authoritarianism can include external threat, fear of communism, economic chaos, or a breakdown in law and order (Das Gupta 1978). The regime turns to the military to help it gain increased powers and to control other political actors.

The military's role changes, then, because it is the institution charged with ensuring that the avenues of political participation are closed and that the mass public is depoliticized. It is responsible for administering martial law and suppressing dissent. It is also a key player because of the rationale that the regime chooses to legitimize itself. If the regime chooses national security and law and order, then it will depend on the military to meet these goals. As a result, the military turns away from more traditional institutional tasks and acquires new tasks that are similar to those of civilian political actors.

Increasing Opposition to the Authoritarian Regime

The regime's reaction to the institution's role change will influence the level of tension within the institutions themselves, as the church and the military decide whether or not to remain in the regime's support coalition. It will also influence the magnitude of change in the level or type of political activity adopted by the church and the military.

The more institutions change their ideologies to adopt Vatican II teachings and the national security state, the more fragmented the institutions themselves will become regarding whether or not to continue supporting the authoritarian regime. Groups within the church will emerge to champion grassroots interests, arguing that its new role of witnessing means that it must ally with the people rather than with the regime. Eventually, groups within the military will emerge who see the institution becoming corrupted by political roles and want it to return to a professional state. In both cases, then, outliers within each institution exert pressure on the institution's hierarchy to stop supporting the regime. Their rationale is institutional interests: to protect and purify the church or the military.

Once the ideological change occurs, the probability increases that the institutions' interests and the regime's behavior will conflict. Because of its new emphasis on social justice, the church is less likely to support a regime that violates human rights. Because of its new emphasis on national security, the military is less likely to support a regime that protects a leader's personal interests.

The more the church and the military oppose the regime, the more its support—and thus its existence—is threatened. If the regime tries to maintain its support coalition, then it will make concessions to the church and military. In this way, conflict is lessened. If, on the other hand, the regime attempts to control these institutions, then conflict escalates.

The second scenario can lead to the church and military becoming openly opposed to the regime. The institutions rethink the value of belonging to the regime's coalition. This reconsideration of coalition membership is significant even if the above change only causes the institutions to move into the semiopposition, rather than the outright opposition. It shows that the potential is there for the institutions to move into open opposition at a later date.

A third scenario is also possible: that the regime will agree to make concessions to institutional interests but will be unable to deliver them. In this scenario, the regime will also lose the support of the church and the military, because they will see the regime as ineffectual and therefore replaceable.

Regime Change and Political Instability

Institutional role change and regime behavior cause the institutions to join the opposition. This change in activity is the result of the erosion of institutional support for the regime, as groups within the institutions break away from their traditional position or from their hierarchy's position. This erosion forces the institutions to defect from the regime in order to regain institutional cohesion. The probability of regime change, then, increases to the extent that groups within the institution break away, openly oppose the regime, and force the institution to defect from the support coalition. If these institutions defect, the coalition may not be strong enough to support the regime by itself. In this way, institutional change and regime behavior cause regime collapse.

Once the regime collapse occurs, the institutions are faced with a dilemma. They are responsible for the regime change and therefore have a vested interest in the formation and stability of the new government. Support from both institutions is crucial for the new democracy. Church support can legitimize the new leader. The church can also stimulate mass support for the new democracy through its grassroots organizations. The military's support is equally important in that its cooperation can guarantee a smooth transition process. Military support also decreases the chances of a new government being overthrown.

However, both institutions are divided as to what should be their actual role in the new government. The cleavage that tore the institutions becomes evident again, as the hierarchies try to pull the institutions back into their traditional roles of supporting the government by not intervening in day-to-day affairs, while the lower levels want to remain in the political arena to influence, or even oppose, the new government. To the extent that the government asks for or relies on their support, both institutions, in turn, will place policy demands on it, either to ensure the democratization process or to protect their own institutional interests. However, both policy positions and institutional interests will be identified in different ways by different subgroups.

The new democratic leader, then, is faced with an enormous challenge. Upon entering office, she must replace elements of the authoritarian regime—the constitution, political institutions, and political actors—with prodemocratic ones. In addition, traditional political actors who were locked out of the political arena will be pressuring the new government for positions and power. What compounds this situation is that social institutions, such as the church and the military, may remain in the political arena. The new leader, then, must not only replace one political system with another but also juggle the conflicting demands of a larger, and more active, group of actors and institutions. Thus, the legacy of authoritarian rule is a fragile democracy.

THE REST OF THE BOOK

This book is divided into three parts. Part 1 lays out the argument, with chapter 2 explaining the institutional changes that the church and the military experience and chapter 3 offering an introduction to the Philippines' version of authoritarianism. Part 2 is an in-depth discussion of the process of institutional change, regime behavior, and regime collapse in the Philippines. Chapters 4 and 5 follow the increasing fragmentation of both the church and the military under the Marcos regime. Chapter 6 focuses on the collapse of the authoritarian regime in the Philippines, and chapter 7 discusses the country's democratization process. Part 3 contains chapter 8, the conclusion, which compares the Philippines' experience with those of Argentina, Brazil, and Chile.

2 The Changing Ideologies and Expanding Roles of the Church and the Military

INTRODUCTION

■ This chapter discusses the changing ideologies and expanding roles of the Roman Catholic church and the military. It documents the church's move from a sacrament-based to a people-based ideology with the introduction of the Second Vatican Council reforms and liberation theology. It focuses on the military's change in protecting the country from external to internal threats, with the emergence of a national security doctrine. These changes significantly affected both the church and the military by fragmenting their membership. This fragmentation increased under authoritarianism, as the institutions were asked to play new roles, and eventually caused the church and the military to oppose and overthrow the authoritarian regime.

The church and the military often initially support authoritarian regimes, in large part because these institutions have interests that align with those of the regimes. As Smith pointed out for Chile, both the church and the military

have preferred order, stability, and harmony among social classes, and both have valued the importance of religious legitimation for the state. Each has long-standing fears of radical political movements, especially those with socialist or Marxist orientations. Each prized tradition, discipline, hierarchical control, and institutional autonomy within its respective organization. (Smith 1986, 270)

Yet, while they are both supporters of the regime, each institution represents different types of support coalition members. The church is a peripheral member of the coalition, while the military is a core supporter. The church agrees with certain policies of the regime but stays outside of the formal structure of government. The military, on the other hand, not only agrees with the regime's policies but also implements them, protecting the regime's very existence.

A further reason the church and the military stand out for comparison is that they each experienced the introduction of a new ideology at around the same time. The Second Vatican Council met in the mid-1960s to discuss reforming church practices, while the national security doctrine was introduced in the late 1950s. As both of these institutions were redefining themselves, they were also both undergoing similar pressures from their members to expand their roles in the political arena.

While these institutions experience similar changes in their ideologies and roles, they have very different goals because of their different clients. As the church adopts liberation theology, it shifts its efforts toward the mass public. As the military adopts a new definition of national security, it becomes the personal tool of the leader or regime, by identifying national interests as regime interests. Thus, while experiencing similar changes, the two institutions are moving in different directions.

THE CHURCH

Although the church has played dramatic roles in the political arenas of Latin America and the Philippines in the seventies and eighties, one should not assume that this marks the church's first incursion into politics. Rather, the church has always been politicized: it has always had political interests and has acted to further them. What has changed over time is the specific role that the church has played and the specific types and levels of activities it has carried out. It has moved from influencing politics as an outsider to being a central actor, and from supporting to opposing the regime.

The Church Prior to Vatican II

For the church, the impetus for this change was the introduction and acceptance of a new ideology, the Vatican II reforms. Prior to Vatican II, the church saw its role as sacrament-based, focused on life hereafter. It was a conservative force, which equated civic obedience and religious obedience (Berryman 1984, 55). Politics means two things to the church: "politics as partisan involvement and public stances, and politics as struggle over power and authority within the ecclesiastical institution" (Levine 1984, 127). Thus, it saw its work as grounded in pastoral activities: saying Mass, conducting charity work, and teaching. Any work that dealt with temporal matters was seen as the role of the laity. Thus, the church was to instill proper values in the laity so that lay people would correctly conduct themselves in the political world.

To protect its role and its activities, the church traditionally allied with the state and with conservative elites (Vallier 1970, 40). Thus, it supported colonialism and postcolonial conservative governments. "During the colonial period, the Church was fully linked with society. It was supported, protected, and given special privileges. In turn, the Church served as an agency of colonial expansion, as an administrative and economic organization, and as a key institution of social control" (Vallier 1967, 194).

When colonial administrations were replaced with local governments, the church allied itself with the conservatives against the liberals (Vallier 1967, 194). In return for its support, the church expected the government to protect its interests (203). Thus, while it became dependent on government and political elites, the church in return gained autonomy in certain areas, such as education (193). Furthermore, it tried to ensure that government and elites would remain favorable to the church, through its socialization in the classroom and from the pulpit (Vallier 1970, 36–37).

The Church After Vatican II

The Second Vatican Council (1962–1965) met to discuss how the church should adapt to the changing world. It felt that the church was becoming increasingly irrelevant to its members because it was ignoring the fundamental conditions of the everyday lives of people. The council moved away from focusing on sacraments and instead focused on changing conditions to bring people's lives closer to social justice. For example, the church began to espouse particular economic policies that were nationalist and pro-worker.

Documents from Vatican II and several papal encyclicals throughout the 1960s have all affirmed the moral necessity for greater restriction on economic competition, increased state planning and public ownership of key resources, worker participation in enterprises, adjustment of international trade agreements, and a more equitable distribution of world resources, to favor the developing countries. (Smith 1975, 6)

Vatican II caused the church to rethink the balance between its moral and its temporal power and to focus on political and social conditions (Smith 1982).

It is clear that as a result of changes in secular society and in the Church itself, the institution has officially legitimized greater differentiation of religious roles and responsibilities; expanded dominant religious goals to incorporate a greater concern for justice and human rights; encouraged more freedom and voluntary commitments among members, and envisioned a more positive and dynamic interaction between Church and world. (Smith 1982, 19)

Vatican II was also decentralizing: it stressed the people of God rather than the institutional church. It stressed that the church must live with the people—the church must have a "preferential option for the poor" (Levine 1981b, 191)—to understand their situation so that the church can be a witness to their suffering. Within the church itself, it reconsidered the division of church work between moral and temporal matters by shifting the church's goal from accepting the social and political status quo (by remaining outside politics) to working for social change. This ideological change to focus on action and the poor influenced the church's organization. "Viewing the Church as a Pilgrim People of God . . . had a profound impact on the structure and meaning of authority in the Church—the kinds of authority, activity, and obedience seen as necessary and legitimate" (Levine 1981a, 36).

Authority became linked with action; not only did this mean that bishops, to retain their authority, would have to engage in social action, but it also meant that traditionally subordinate religious members, including lay workers, also possessed authority to the extent that they were active. Thus, the ideological change in the church had a corresponding decentralizing and democratizing effect on its organization.

After Vatican II, Latin American priests began to critique accepted views that economic development was benign (Berryman 1984, 27); liberation theology was one of the results of this debate (Dodson 1979a; Boff 1986; Boff and Boff 1986; Brunello 1986; Berryman 1987; Pottenger 1989). Liberation theology

is a profoundly *ecclesiastical* theology, worked out in intimate, concrete communion with the Christian community, its pastors and its faithful alike. Liberation theology emerges as a service of expression and explanation of the faith, hope, and charity of the community of Christians. Second, the theology of liberation is an altogether *concrete* theology. Its intent is to "think the life problems of the people of God" in order to resolve these problems with the leaven of the Gospel. (Boff and Boff 1986, 18)

Regional Latin American bishops' meetings held in Medellin (1968) and Puebla (1979) were aimed at identifying the sources of social injustice, stressing domestic political structures and international economic structures (Smith 1975, 7).

The Church, which from colonial times had enjoyed significant material privileges resulting from a close association with the established order, officially and publicly went on record condemning the injustices inherent in existing social and economic structures and placed its moral weight on the side of those seeking major reforms to benefit the poor. (Smith 1975, 8)

Levine points out that the meeting at Puebla stressed four interrelated points. First, the church must move away from sacrament-based work and instead refocus on the Bible. Second, it must make the Bible relevant to the lives of people, especially those who suffer from social or political injustice. Third, it must espouse evangelization, even if such action creates a break between church and state. Fourth, evangelization was to be achieved via grassroots groups attached to the church, which would work for social justice, pastoral action, and the explicit "preferential option for the poor" (Levine 1981b, 190–91).

The above discussion focuses church and politics research onto two main points. First, the church has experienced a change in its ideology, due to Vatican II, to increase its focus on action. This ideological change has caused the church to redefine its political role. Second, the messages of social action and the preferential option for the poor imply a need to change church organization by decentralizing authority. This pressure for organizational change has caused the church to redefine its hierarchy of obedience.

Political Activities of the Church After Vatican II

The tension that the church experienced between the new ideology of Vatican II and the institution's organization influenced the scope of its political activites. As congregations accepted Vatican II reforms, they focused more on the lives of the poor. Initial changes in activity, then, are shifts from sacramental work to evangelical work. As evangelical work is carried out, churches shift again to more openly political behavior, lobbying for social reform and opposing authoritarian regimes.

The introduction of Vatican II reforms and liberation theology did not cause an immediate transformation of church roles and behavior around the world. Rather, churches differed by country as to when they adopted the new ideology. The natural inclination of the church hierarchy would be to resist the Vatican II reforms because the changes would diminish its role, specifically its traditional control over the ideology and behavior of the institution (Vallier 1967, 203). Whether or not the churches would shift their support for Vatican II reforms depends on the positions of the different groups within it. The church is not a homogeneous institution (Levine 1981a, 9; Smith 1982, 62). Rather, its "monolithic structure hides its heterogeneity and decentralization" (Levine 1981a, 9). There are always groups within the church pushing for different approaches.

There are two models of the church, showing the effect of roles on activities.

The first builds around ecclesiastical structures, with average members in a distinct and subordinate relation to clergy. The pervasive stress on hierarchy, organizational unity, and clerical dominance converges in a style in which goals and orientations flow from the "church" to "the world." The very use of these terms stresses separation: society is to be suffused with Christian principles; the world is to be reconquered for the church. The second model builds religious unity on the solidarity of community and shared experience. Institutional unity thus rests on social unity, with the stress on homogeneous, class-based groups. The emphasis on solidarity undercuts clerical dominance and reduces the centrality of ecclesiastical structures. The church is part of the world, and orientations are sought in daily experience. Action may thus stem from social analysis, without the mediation of authoritative doctrine. Society is remade, not rechristianized. (Levine 1986, 189)

While churches may accept Vatican II reforms, they may implement them at different speeds or strengths. On the one hand, countries may be like Colombia, where the church hierarchy implemented Vatican II while simultaneously trying to delete any class references. Thus, their activities were conducted under strict hierarchical control to ensure church unity (Levine 1986, 194). Because the bishops feared class division and politics, "it comes as no surprise that Catholic organizations [in Colombia] should stress loyalty, control, and a restricted range of 'safe' activities" (198). Thus, the church in Colombia shifted its activities from social action, charity, and Catholic Action movements, prior to Vatican II, to the creation of distinct groups directly under the control of the hierarchy created for pastoral and political work (196).

On the other hand, countries may follow the path of Brazil, where the church hierarchy took the lead in defining liberation theology. Unlike in Colombia, the Brazilian church encouraged popular organizations and decentralized church structures and power. Eventually, these local organizations became the basis of grassroots organizations that openly opposed the authoritarian regime (Levine and Mainwaring 1989, 235).

After Vatican II, pastoral work focused on the church sharing the experiences of the poor. In Nicaragua, El Salvador, and Guatemala, where the institutional church was weak, the implementation of Vatican II–related activities was due to foreign priests and local priests who had studied abroad. Their activities ranged from development-oriented projects to conscientization (learning that God supports the poor) and the creation of Basic Christian Communities (BCCs) (Berryman 1984, 223–25). These communities created a structure that allowed for church members to live with the poor and use this sharing of day-to-day life as the basis of a dialogue with the poor, relating the Gospel to their world. Communities were initially created under the aegis of the institutional church (Levine and Mainwaring 1989, 205).

However, these communities had the potential for becoming popularly controlled, since the lay members themselves were encouraged to set their agendas. This local control was significant, because for "the first time the locus of decision, conflict, and initiative has shifted to groups that poor people play a key role in establishing and maintaining" (Levine and Mainwaring 1989,

204). This decentralization also shifted the "norms of power and authority *within* the churches" by increasing the influence of local church members themselves (204). Power was placed in the hands of the laity: people were encouraged to discuss the Gospel through their own experiences, to relate the Gospel to their day-to-day lives, to come up with solutions to their problems, and to lead the efforts in solving them (Berryman 1984, 31).

One could argue that the proper role of priests and sisters was simply consciousness-raising and evangelization and that the people were making political options on their own. But that might seem as though the church's pastoral agents were abandoning people when evangelization led to risk and danger. Did not pastoral commitment imply a duty to stay with people and accompany them throughout their journey? If so, what were the implications for the relationship between the church (pastoral agents and CEBs) and the popular organizations? (Berryman 1986, 67)

Furthermore, this decentralization had the potential not only to conscienticize and organize the mass public, but also to compel the church as an institution to oppose the regime. Actual church responses varied by country. For example, the Guatemalan hierarchy tried to neither support nor oppose the regime, while the Nicaraguan hierarchy took a strong and unified position in opposing the regime (Berryman 1984, 225). However, even if church reaction to the regime is muted, its grassroots experience sets the groundwork for shifting its support in the future (Levine and Mainwaring 1989, 207). Thus, the move from conscientization to organization sets up the possibility of a corresponding move from identifying the root of the problem as local landlords to criticizing economic and political structures at the national level (Berryman 1984, 31).

To some extent those who blamed the church for fomenting Marxism were right—the popular organizations often seemed to spring out of CEBs. For the people at the village level it seemed hard (and perhaps not important) to distinguish between the CEB and the organization.

Hence Archbishop Romero felt that he had to insist on the differences between the two, while nonetheless stressing the positive relationship. This symbiotic relationship posed new problems, especially for pastoral workers: should priests and sisters simply defend people's rights to organize, or should they accompany them in their struggle, even joining the organizations? (Berryman 1986, 76)

As the church tries to change the way people think about religion and apply it to their own lives, it will also engender a change in itself as an institution (Levine and Mainwaring 1989, 206). One of the most important changes, which this book follows, is the effect of church activity on church-state relations. BCCs, by organizing people to act to help themselves and by relating the roots of the problems to current economic and political structures, can act as avenues for church members to speak out against the regime. Such activities include documenting human rights violations, coordinating activities with opposition groups, and joining guerrilla groups (Berryman 1984, 223–25).

The Authoritarian Regime and the Church

When authoritarianism is installed, the regime's goal is the constriction of institutions and avenues of participation. While an authoritarian regime changes political institutions and groups in order to control them, it will not necessarily be successful. The regime, in particular, is constantly trying to control those institutions that remain independent, through the use of carrots and sticks. On the one hand, it tries to coopt institutions by building its support coalition to include them. In this way, certain societal sectors, such as business or the church, attain avenues for political input and preferential policy. On the other hand, in order to gain their compliance, the regime also threatens these independent institutions, such as the church, with penalties if they try to oppose authoritarianism (Linz 1973, 191–92). In the Philippines, for example, Marcos threatened to tax church property and allow divorce and birth control as a way of curbing increasing church opposition to the regime (Wurfel 1977, 17–18).

Although the regime is trying to depoliticize the population, it is not always successful. One possibility is that the mass public will not be depoliticized but rather will shift its focus of demands from traditional to nontraditional political institutions (Scott 1985). This aspect of authoritarianism has relevance for the church. As usual avenues for participation are blocked off, such as when the legislature is closed, people turn to the church to champion their demands and protect their interests. The church becomes a natural candidate for this new role because of its symbolic role as a protector of people and as a moral force in society. The church's role, then, is changed dramatically by the public's transference of their demands from Congress to the church.

It is not surprising that the mass public would turn to the church as an avenue of political action. Often, the church is one of the few independent institutions under such a regime, after the regime closes Congress, bans political parties, and institutes martial law. The church becomes a symbol of independence from, if not opposition to, the regime. This position places stress upon the church. We see that in Latin America there was a simultaneous change in both the church and governments, as the churches adopted a more decentralized ideology and regimes became authoritarian. As churches encouraged action at the local level, "popular religious groups became targets of official violence because any autonomous organization was suspect in the eyes of fearful elites." In "all the cases where CEBs later became prominent, political closure was decisive in magnifying their impact as CEBs became the only available vehicles for popular organization" (Levine and Mainwaring 1989, 211).

The church's experience under authoritarianism, juxtaposed with its new ideology, which focuses on church activism in the political arena, causes the church to slowly change its activity. It becomes more overtly political and moves away from supporting the authoritarian regime. The more it changes to align with the new ideology, the more the church as an institution, rather than only individual members, overtly opposes an authoritarian regime.

After Vatican II, church and state interests were no longer naturally aligned, creating the opportunity for the church to act against the state to support its own institutional interests (Levine 1984, 122). The new ideology's emphasis of linking the Gospels to everyday political and economic issues immediately brings church members, groups, and the institution itself into potential conflict with the regime, since such discussions revolve around morality and liberation and a call for action. The institutional church, then, faces a quandary. It can try to protect itself by not critiquing the regime, but it will not be following a prophetic role. Or it can follow a prophetic role, critique the regime, and have its members persecuted (Comblin 1984, 173). Thus, the church is faced with internal tension and polarization as local groups more and more adopt a prophetic role.

[Political] activism, conflict with the state, and increasingly violent oppression and abuse by public authorities has led many in the churches to new reflections on the political implications of faith and the religious meaning of political action in contemporary Latin America. Of course, oppression and violence are nothing new. But now they are increasingly directed at the churches, and the historical conjunction of expanding authoritarian regimes with religious institutions and individuals seeking to express their faith through social and political action has magnified vastly the importance of commitment and activism as dimensions of religious experience. In the process, a great deal of borrowing and mutual influence (both unconscious and deliberate) is visible between religion and politics, to the point where conventional distinctions have become increasingly blurred. (Levine 1981b, 186)

Furthermore, this change in the roles the church plays can continue after the overthrow of the authoritarian regime. When a new democracy is introduced, the church may withdraw its membership from the opposition, but it will not necessarily end its concern for social issues or its political involvement. Indeed, rank-and-file members of the institution, who are engaged in grassroots concerns on a daily basis, will continue to pressure government for social and economic change, to parallel the political change that the country has experienced.

Thus, even "if 'power' is not 'taken,' the experience of discussion, organization, struggle, and action can nurture an independent popular consciousness and in this way make possible continued resistance to authority and sustained struggle for change" (Levine and Mainwaring 1989, 207). To this end, BCCs may be used as an avenue to increase and channel grassroots political involvement (Mainwaring 1989, 175). Such involvement can range from organizing people to address local issues to encouraging people to vote for the candidates of specific political parties (179). Thus, the church's experiences will have a long-term effect, even if the hierarchy tries to pull the church back to its pre-authoritarian position that politics is the domain of the laity. Given the Vatican II reforms and the institution's experience under authoritarianism, the church may temporarily withdraw after the installation of a democratic government, but it will be ready to undertake political action as it deems necessary.

Thus, as the church implements its new ideology it moves closer to the mass public as it identifies with and works for its day-to-day interests. With the imposition of authoritarianism, the church's ideological shift is reinforced, as it becomes a political channel for the mass public to critique the regime and as it acts to protect the political interests of the public. As a result of both of these factors, the church finds itself increasingly fulfilling an opposition role, to the point where it actively works to oust the regime. Once a democratic government is installed, the church will not necessarily retreat; rather, the long-term effect is continued political activity.

THE MILITARY

Like the church, the military has always played a role in politics in Latin America, both directly in politics through intervention and indirectly through influencing leaders. However, the military has also experienced a role change, due to the rise of a national security doctrine. Like the church, then, the military has moved increasingly from the role of an influencer to a central actor, and from supporting to opposing the regime.

The Military Prior to the National Security Doctrine

The role of the military changed significantly with the introduction of the national security doctrine. The traditional role of the military ranged from professionalism, whereby the institution followed civilian supremacy, to intervention, where the military would overthrow and replace one civilian government with another one. However, in the latter case, while the military would intervene against a government, it did not consider itself a legitimate ruler.

Under professionalism, the military accepted or acceded to civilian supremacy. This acceptance was due in part to the military seeing certain institutional benefits in being "above politics" (Janowitz 1964, 65). In this role, the

Identification of the military with national pride and honor creates a sort of political aloofness on their part, based on the conviction that politics is beneath military honor. They stand for consensus; politics implies competition, rivalry, and conflict between interest groups. They symbolize the interest of the whole nation; politics seeks the interests of particular groups within the nation. (Khuri 1982, 14)

However, the tradition of supporting the government does not mean that the military remained completely out of the political realm. The military has always followed a middle path between the two models of professionalism and politicization. It saw its work as primarily supporting the government and protecting the country from external threat. Military officers were powerful political actors behind the scenes, often more able to permeate the state than traditional interest groups (Hyman 1972, 411). Thus, they also filled the role of influencer. Indeed, one theorist argues that the military's presence in the political realm is so pervasive that the term intervention may not be useful in describing military behavior, "owing to the frequency of military political action, increased participation of military officers in government, and the realization that the military may be considered a legitimate political power group in developing countries" (Nunn 1975, 272n2).

In Latin America, the military "were in fact not strictly professional, no matter what the law said; rather, they were highly political groups. They 'deliberated' on all matters, particularly 'on matters relating to the service,' that is, on budgets, manpower, [and] equipment needs" (Lieuwen 1962, 150).

Furthermore, the military felt justified in playing a political role not only when their overt institutional interests—such as resources—were at stake, but even when they decided that the nation's interests were also being harmed (Needler 1975).

Accordingly, the military arrogated to itself the power of deciding when constitutional rights had been violated and when the time had arrived to enforce the law. Though there were obvious cases where military intervention was needed to curb irresponsible military and civilian politicos, it was highly questionable, in most instances, whether military intervention was in fact justified. On all too many occasions the armed forces acted arbitrarily and in utter defiance of the duly constituted authorities and the popular will. (Lieuwen 1962, 151–52)

However, when the military did intervene and take over government, it did so from a position of administrative weakness, since "military training did little to equip an officer with the skills necessary for running a modern state" (Lieuwen 1962, 152). Thus, it was common to see military interventions but not longstanding military governments: it would be a moderating power rather than a ruling one.

The military's sense of professionalism and influence was expandable, allowing it to institute a coup against the government because of its belief that it was charged with protecting national interests (Needler 1975). This concept of national interests could be defined in several ways. First, the formal role of many militaries in Latin America included the idea that they were to protect the country's constitution, or to follow the orders of the civilian leaders "within the limits of the law," thus potentially placing them at odds with the civilian rulers and allowing them leeway to intervene in politics (Wesson and Fleischer 1983, 129). Second, many officers in Latin American militaries saw their traditional role to include protecting the country from its own leaders (McCann 1979, 509). Third, in Brazil in the 1930s, there was the belief that military intervention in politics was part of the military's legitimate role, but only if the military was acting as one unit rather than promoting the political ambitions of individual officers and only if the military's action would protect their institutional interests or order in the country (519–20). Fourth, the military was often encouraged to intervene in politics, either indirectly, as a result of having its institution politicized by a leader, or directly, by being asked to take on such nontraditional military tasks as industrialization. Fifth, civilians would "knock on the barracks door" and ask the military to overthrow government (Wesson and Fleischer 1983, 130).

However, the military also has selfish reasons for intervening against a civilian government. Specifically, the military will institute a coup to protect its institutional interests (Needler 1975; North and Nunn 1978). Thus, the military will intervene if it believes that the leader is harming the military by politicizing or constraining the institution. Civilian politicization of the military includes leaders undermining the line of command or interfering in the promotion process. Examples of constraining the military would be reducing its budget or denying it equipment or freedom of action deemed necessary by the military to successfully carry out its duties (Needler 1975, 89–71). Often, though, the military will point to national reasons as a higher rationale for its intervention, so as to gain societal support for its actions.

The Military Under the National Security Doctrine

The introduction of a national security doctrine created a "new professionalism" within the military (Stepan 1971). This new ideology within the institution emerged in the late 1950s, as United States military assistance programs to Third World countries began to stress counterinsurgency training (Stepan 1977, 50). The idea behind the shift was that Third World governments faced a greater threat to their national security from internal rather than external forces. Thus, it was believed that a retraining of the military, through the introduction of a new professionalism, would strengthen democratic governments in the Third World. However, the actual result was the reverse: such training shifted the military away from civilian supremacy and toward the military assumption of political positions.

Under the old professionalism, the training that the military is given and the roles it is expected to play are focused on external security. Under new professionalism, the military shifts its focus to internal security through expanding its training to include civilian managerial skills, such as socioeconomic development and nation building. This training is considered an additional tactic that the military can then implement to encourage or force the population to shift its loyalty from guerrilla forces to the government. These skills trigger a corresponding expansion in the type and scope of the roles that the military fills. It takes on traditionally civilian roles in the public sector (such as positions in local government and ministries) and the private sector (such as managerial positions in industries). The military's scope of action is significantly widened, as any role that can be related to domestic law and order can be potentially entered into by the military (Stepan 1977, 52).

This role expansion politicizes the military in two significant ways. First, it brings the military into roles traditionally held by politicians and bureaucrats. This expansion legitimizes, in the military's own eyes, its ability to rule. Second, it causes the military to judge the success of the civilian government in decreasing insurgency levels and in ruling effectively, because the military begins to rethink its initial belief in civilian supremacy. The military considers overthrowing the government and taking its place, thus becoming not only a moderating force but a ruling one.

This new ideology gives the military the necessary "change in structural, motivational, perceptual, intellectual, and corporate orientations" to allow military members to intervene in politics and stay there as regime rulers (Perlmutter 1980b, 98–99). They see their roles expanded to include the stabilization of politics (Perlmutter 1982, 314). Thus, they see the existence of unstable governments unable to cope with crises as their opportunity to act (Perlmutter 1982, 312; Cohen 1987, 53).

When the military institutes a coup and remains in the political arena, it can gain support through an alliance with several potential actors. Technocrats are one possible group (Perlmutter 1980a, 238; Linz 1973; O'Donnell 1979, 83). Because the military's new training includes courses on socioeconomic development and nation building, the military and technocrats have more in common now. They would also share a similar approach to societal problems, in that they would prefer a reorganization of government that streamlines decision making by centralizing power (O'Donnell 1979, 84).

Political Activities of the Military Under the National Security Doctrine

Like the church, the military begins to change its activities to correspond with its new ideology and its experiences under authoritarianism. As the military adopts the national security doctrine, it takes on traditionally civilian roles in the government. Thus, it moves from more professional to more political activities. As it fills government roles, it shifts to more open political behavior and increasingly opposes the authoritarian regime.

The rise of the national security doctrine had external and internal support. Externally, Third World countries accepted aid from the United States as a way to strengthen their national security, while the armed forces saw it as a way to expand their institutional resources. The United States created the Military Assistance Program (MAP) in the early 1950s as a mechanism to aid anticommunism efforts by Third World armed forces. MAP gave grant assistance to countries for "military equipment, services, training, and administrative support" (Hammond et al. 1983, 127). The United States also set up the International Military Education and Training (IMET) Program as a less costly way to train and set up ties with Third World military officers (128).

Military training was extended to include police and paramilitary personnel, and aid also included U.S. military advisors. The idea behind the program was that such grants would be used to help the countries internally, against insurgency (Klare and Arnson 1981, 44). For example, after World War II, the Brazilian military's mission shifted from external security to internal security. Brazil's external security was defended through an alliance with the United States, and its ability to conduct military operations in Latin America was constrained by its membership in the Organization of American States. Thus, military officers shifted their focus to internal security (McCann 1980, 124).

There were also internal stimuli to support the national security state, specifically from the armed forces themselves. Besides traditional military training, the armed forces were also encouraged to fight insurgency through implementing civic action programs. Such public works programs as "the construction of roads, schools, hospitals, irrigation systems, [and] power plants" were heralded as aiding counterinsurgency because they had the potential to redirect mass support away from guerrilla movements and toward the government (Feldman 1982, 332). In Argentina, MAP funding was used for civic action programs in the two years prior to the 1966 authoritarian regime (330).

Thus, the military's training began to be expanded from strictly military or strategic concerns to include skills that were previously monopolized by civilians. In Latin America, an "officer's professional training often equipped him for the ministry of communications or of public works or other technical posts" (Lieuwen 1960, 139). In Brazil, "almost all military officers agreed that since labor, fiscal, educational, and other problems were intrinsic to the security of the nation, it was legitimate and necessary for military men to concern themselves with these areas" (Stepan 1971, 186). Lieuwen points out that the military set up communications lines in Brazil, Peru, and Bolivia and built roads, schools, and hospitals in Mexico and Argentina (Lieuwen 1960, 139). In Argentina, the military was also involved in the management of its mining and arms industries (Feldman 1982, 332).

Such training also included specific administrative skills, which the military realized it had lacked in the past when it had intervened in government. The military received advanced technical training in economic development and business management (including anti-inflation and fiscal policies), agrarian reform, and voting and elections (Kossok 1972, 391; McCann 1980, 124). In Brazil, military officers were placed on detached status to take development-oriented positions in the bureaucracy and in business (McCann 1980, 125).

Because of the new training, the military became convinced that it could fill government roles traditionally held by civilians. As military officers took on more activities, their sense of empowerment grew. Thus, in countries like Brazil and Argentina, the military took over government and stayed in power by establishing military regimes. In Brazil, the military officers

had come to believe that, in comparison to the civilian politicians, they now had constructed the correct doctrines of national security and development, possessed the trained cadres to implement these doctrines, and had the institutional force to impose their solution to the crisis in Brazil. Thus, after overthrowing the civilian president in 1964, the Brazilian military did not return power to new civilian groups, as they had in 1930, 1945, 1954, and 1955, but assumed political power themselves for the first time in the century. (Stepan 1977, 58)

As the military responds to its new, political roles, it will begin to change as an institution. Specifically, the activities that the military takes on change its self-image and therefore its relations with the authoritarian regime. By entering into the political arena and filling such traditional civilian tasks as building schools and administering public corporations, it sees itself as a legitimate political leader, not just as a political actor. As it fills such roles, it also begins to compare itself with other actors. Such comparison causes the military to view itself more and more favorably and to judge the authoritarian regime more and more harshly. Thus, over time, the military begins to oppose the regime.

The Authoritarian Regime and the Military

The authoritarian regime needs the military as a support base. The military is usually integral to the regime's basis of legitimacy, which can include law and order or counterinsurgency. It is also the institution charged with ensuring that the avenues of political participation are closed and that the mass public is depoliticized. Finally, because the regime closes traditional political institutions and tries to control mass participation, it depends on the military to administer martial law and suppress dissent.

The military becomes integral to the authoritarian regime in part because of the regime's rationale for existing. Often, the regime will choose an issue related to national security to legitimize itself, such as the decline of law and order or the rise of a Communist threat. There is a constant tension between the regime establishing such a rationale for its existence and successfully obtaining societal support. If the rationale does not successfully legitimize the regime, then the regime must find some way to coerce the population to obey.

By instituting martial law, the regime closes traditional political institutions, creating a vacuum. Labor unions, political parties, and other traditional social groups are often outlawed, leaving the military as one of the few institutions capable of concerted action. The regime relies more and more on the military to take on the political tasks once filled by these institutions. The military's role changes dramatically, then, as the regime relies on it for support.

The regime's law and order goals increase the role of the military because it becomes a fundamental protector of the regime's existence. In this manner, the military becomes identified with political, rather than professional, interests. It becomes identified with protecting the leaders of the regime rather than the constitution or the country as a whole.

The more the military shifts away from professionalism, the more diverse are the tasks it takes on and, therefore, the more likely are cleavages to emerge within the institution. When the military is professional, there is only one role—that of following civilian authority. There is a clear basis for making decisions such as promotion: they can be made on the basis of professional performance. However, as roles expand to include political tasks, the bases for such decisions become less obvious and more conflictual. Two tracks emerge—the professional track and the political track—and military personnel are forced to choose between the two. This choice creates tensions within the institution as it becomes fragmented and as the groups begin to compete with each other for limited promotion slots and resources.

The military's adoption of the national security doctrine and its experience under authoritarianism pull the institution in different directions. The new ideology encourages the military to support the creation of an authoritarian regime because it will benefit from the change. The military gains an expansion of roles, an increase in resources, and an enhancement of status. However, once the authoritarian regime is in place, the military slowly realizes that the change from democracy to authoritarianism is not free of cost. While the institution receives certain benefits from the regime, it also experiences significant internal stress while carrying out its new duties. Professional members of the military begin to question the initial assumption that military men can administer and rule as well as bureaucrats and politicians. They begin to pressure the institution to reverse its decision to intervene in politics.

As the military adopts more roles, then, it loses its unity. Professional members of the military see the institution becoming corrupted by political roles and want it to return to its preauthoritarian professional role to protect and purify the military as an institution. This group may see its interests served only by an end to the authoritarian regime. Internal conflicts within the military, caused by the expansion of roles demanded of it by the authoritarian regime, may therefore lead parts of the military to oppose the regime. If this group wins the internal struggle, the institution as a whole will turn against the very regime that relies so heavily on it to remain in power. However, once a democratic government is installed, the military will not necessarily remain outside of politics. Politically oriented military officers will continue to push for role expansion, and the military as an institution will continue to act to defend its own interests. Thus, the long-term effect for the military, as well as the church, is continued political activity.

3 Authoritarianism in the Philippines

INTRODUCTION

■ Authoritarianism is made up of four components, and each component was applied by Marcos to the Philippines. Authoritarianism is a political system that focuses on constraining political participation while simultaneously ensuring mass subservience to the regime. It is characterized by four components: (1) constraints on political institutions, (2) a basis for the regime's legitimacy, (3) constraints on the mass public, and (4) ill-defined executive power (Linz 1964, 297).

Authoritarianism was installed in the Philippines in 1972. From 1946 until 1972, the Philippines had practiced presidential democracy. Its brand of democracy was influenced formally by the constitution of the United States, since the Philippines had been an American colony from 1898 until 1946, and informally by the elite practices of the Spanish administrators, since it had been a Spanish colony from the 1600s until 1898. President Ferdinand E. Marcos declared martial law in 1972 and ruled as an authoritarian leader until 1986. It is no coincidence that martial law was declared in 1972, since Marcos had already held the office of the president for two consecutive terms and was therefore ineligible to run for the presidency in the 1973 elections.

CONSTRAINTS ON POLITICAL INSTITUTIONS

Authoritarian regimes constrain institutions and groups—such as legislatures, political parties, and interest groups—from participation in politics (Linz 1964, 298). By limiting their independence, the regime hopes both to increase its own control in diminishing the number and strength of its competitors and to limit demands by controlling the avenues of participation.

The declaration of martial law allowed Marcos to close Congress (Abueva 1979, 49). From 1972 to 1978, he exercised legislative powers himself, through the release of executive orders. In 1978, Marcos installed an interim National Assembly (the interim Batasang Pambansa or IBP), which was created through amendments to the 1973 constitution. This legislature was greatly reduced in powers compared with the old Congress. It could only deliberate on bills submitted to it by the cabinet (such as the budget) or which concerned local issues (such as the creation or renaming of universities). This body was more striking for the powers it did not have, including the power to ratify treaties or to choose or remove the prime minister (Catilo and Tapales 1988, 157–59). The interim National Assembly was also under Marcos's personal control, since the president also served as prime minister. In this capacity, Marcos could close the IBP whenever he deemed that "it was not doing its job properly or if he decided there was a national emergency" (Noble 1986, 97). Thus, its purpose was not to enhance participation but to legitimize his regime (Machado 1979, 134).

Martial law was nominally lifted in 1981. In 1984, the regular National Assembly (the Batasang Pambansa or BP), was created. The National Assembly had more legislative power, such as the power to veto presidential legislation, to declare war, to amend the constitution, and to impeach government officials. A greater percentage of its members were elected, compared with the interim legislature. This body was headed by a prime minister who was separate from the president but nominated by him (Catilo and Tapales 1988, 157–59). However, presidential legislation, such as executive orders or presidential decrees, remained legally binding.

Marcos's authoritarian regime also constricted the activities of political parties. When Congress was closed in 1972, elections and, therefore, political parties were suspended. In 1978, when elections were held to select representatives to the interim National Assembly, Marcos created an umbrella organization, the New Society Movement (the Kilusang Bagong Lipunan or KBL), which monopolized electoral politics from 1978 to 1986. Although ostensibly a political party, it was in effect a personal campaign organization for Marcos. Thus, even though the New Society Movement was formed in 1978, it was not formally organized until 1980 (Wurfel 1988, 130). The party became Marcos's martial law patronage network, in that politicians knew that if they wanted to have influence in the regime, they would have to be a member of the New Society Movement.

Opposition parties, when allowed to exist, offered at best a symbolic challenge to Marcos's hold on electoral politics. LABAN, a party consisting of pre–martial law politicians in the Manila area and including Benigno Aquino, ran in the 1978 elections on the MetroManila ballot but did not gain any seats, according to the official tally. Pusyon Bisaya, a regional political party from the Visayas, received thirteen seats in the 1978 elections but was perceived as a loyal opposition party whose existence lent the appearance of competitive elections. UNIDO, an umbrella opposition organization led by Salvador Laurel and other politicians who split from the New Society Movement in the late 1970s, did receive seats in the 1984 elections. The most serious resistance to the Marcos regime was rooted in the Communist Party of the Philippines, which was declared illegal. The CPP waged its guerrilla war through its military arm, the New People's Army, and carried out its political fight, especially its calls for election boycotts, through coalition groups like the National Democratic Front (Tancangco 1988, 95–101; Wurfel 1988, 133). Yet, however much symbolic power or moral legitimacy any of these parties were able to achieve, they were unable to challenge the hold that Marcos held over political organizations.

A similar pattern of constraining access to political organizations was evident in the Philippines with the regime's restructuring of interest groups so as to control them. In the political sphere, besides creating the New Society Movement, Marcos tried to circumvent traditional politicians by having the Department of Local Government and Community Development act as a peak organization and encouraging people to participate through their *barangay,* or local assemblies. In this way, Marcos created a direct link from his cabinet to the local governments, which isolated politicians and bureaucrats whom he did not trust. In the economic sphere, peak organizations were created for labor (the Trade Union Congress of the Philippines) and business (the Employers Confederation of the Philippines). In the professional sector, a similar organization was created for the media (the Philippine Council for Print Media), and attempts were made to duplicate this process for other professions, such as the Integrated Bar of the Philippines (Stauffer 1977, 398–400).

As we see, the Marcos regime in the Philippines did have the first component of authoritarianism, that of constraints on the political institutions. After the declaration of martial law, Marcos closed the Congress and reorganized the government to monopolize avenues of power. The following discussion shows that the Marcos regime was characterized by a particular justification for its installation.

BASIS FOR LEGITIMACY

An authoritarian regime uses an emotional justification for the regime's existence (Linz 1964, 302). It identifies the regime's basis for legitimacy with easily recognizable societal problems, such as underdevelopment or insurgency, and projects the regime as a necessary evil to successfully address such problems. Through the identification of specific problems, the regime hopes to build if not acceptance then acquiescence to its constraint of the political arena and suppression of mass participation.

Even before September 1972, Marcos intimated that he was considering implementing martial law and started laying the groundwork for its introduction and acceptance. By the early

1970s, there was a general sense that immediate social change was necessary. For example, a Constitutional Convention (Con-Con) was called in 1971 to overhaul the constitution to address nationalist needs and socioeconomic crises. Marcos took advantage of this sense of impending social crisis by calling for a "revolution from above" that would reform society while simultaneously barring the Left from taking power (Abueva 1979, 32).

Marcos pointed to the need for strong power within the executive in order to introduce and successfully implement such reform. In particular, he called for the need for discipline within the country. This call for discipline was used to justify not only the implementation of martial law but also the corresponding end to democratic practices and the use of human rights abuses to instill obedience (Abueva 1979, 35).

To legitimize his regime, Marcos claimed that there existed a serious threat to national security. He pointed to the collapse of law and order in the country, using as examples the bombing at Plaza Miranda and the rise in warlord armies. He charged that the government risked being overthrown by various insurgency groups, including students, the Communist New People's Army, and the Muslim secessionist movement (the Moro Nationalist Liberation Front or MNLF) in Mindanao.

Marcos tried to alleviate citizens' fears over martial law by stressing the legality of his proclamation. Thus, he used the term *constitutional authoritarianism* to describe his regime. This term, it was hoped, would give Marcos two advantages. First, it would imply that the centralization and expansion of his powers were implemented in accordance with the constitution, and therefore limited in scope. Second, it implied that, since Marcos had not formally ignored the letter of the law, he would return the country to democracy once the crisis had ended.

To increase support for the regime, Marcos pointed out that the martial law period would also be used to introduce socioeconomic reforms. Marcos promised to build a "new society" by simultaneously achieving economic development and social justice. Thus, he proposed a government reorganization program to encourage economic planning, a Land to the Tiller Program, increased foreign borrowing to finance government projects, and the attraction of foreign investment (Rosenberg 1979, 17; Wurfel 1977, 9).

In accordance with this idea of martial law as an opportunity for reform, Marcos introduced a new slogan for his regime: *Isang Bansa, Isang Diwa,* or One Nation, One Spirit. In this way, Marcos was trying to use a carrot and stick approach. On the one hand, he pointed to the Communist threat as an immediate social crisis that required the installation of an authoritarian regime, because only through such centralization of power, Marcos argued, could he protect the country. On the other hand, while the country was under martial law, Marcos offered to use his enhanced executive powers to implement socioeconomic reforms.

Thus, the Marcos regime fits the second component of authoritarianism. In particular, it used a two-tiered basis of legitimacy—the threat of insurgents overthrowing the government and the prospects for socioeconomic reform—to justify its installation. As we will see in the next section, the regime also constrained individual political participation.

Constraints on the Mass Public

Authoritarian regimes depress the mass public's level of political participation in order to depoliticize the population (Linz 1964, 304). The regime does call for the mass public to participate occasionally, as it needs a facade of popular support. However, such participation is heavily controlled by the regime and is not meant to be a true transmission of mass demands. Furthermore, antiregime participation is forbidden, and the regime uses repressive tactics against its opponents to dissuade them from acting and to discourage potential allies from joining them.

In the Philippines, the declaration of martial law in 1972 also created low mobilization through the suspension of elections.

From 1972 to 1978, Marcos used the referenda process to strictly control and manipulate public participation. In this manner, he was able to gain public "approval" for such crucial decisions as the ratification of the 1973 constitution, the continuation of martial law, the cancellation of the scheduled 1973 elections, the delay in opening the legislature, and his own continuation in power (Abueva 1979, 50–51; Del Carmen 1979, 92–94; Wurfel 1988, 117–22).

Elections were eventually held in 1978, to fill the newly created interim National Assembly. However, due to unfair campaign rules and electoral fraud, the opposition received only fourteen out of 165 elected slots (Machado 1979, 134). In 1984, the next scheduled parliamentary election, the opposition was able to increase its seats to sixty-one, yet this was still only one-third of the positions up for election (Malin 1985, 200). (For the 1984 parliamentary elections, Marcos raised the number of electable positions from 165 to 183.) For the 1981 presidential elections, Marcos tried to outwit the opposition's call for a boycott by encouraging a retired brigadier general to run as the opposition's candidate. Marcos claimed that 88 percent of the votes were in favor of his reelection (Wurfel 1988, 253).

Not surprisingly, both the referenda and the election procedures were set up in such a way as to deny real mass participation. Tactics such as voice votes, voting by show of hands, flying voters, ballot buying, ballot box stuffing, and miscounting ensured that Marcos and his party won. By the early 1980s, the mass public was less willing to ignore such tactics, as is evidenced by a strong boycott movement for the 1981 presidential elections, where it was estimated that over 50 percent of the registered voters refused to vote (Wurfel 1988, 253).

Marcos tried to depoliticize Philppine society not only through the control and manipulation of referenda and elections but also through the implementation of political repression. The declaration of martial law allowed the regime to suspend habeas corpus and detain people suspected of conducting subversive acts, with subversion loosely understood to mean any form of opposition, including nonviolent protest (Amnesty International 1982, 9). The day after martial law was declared, the military arrested suspected opposition members, including prominent politicians, journalists, and labor leaders (Abueva 1979, 35–36). By 1977, over seventy thousand people had been detained (Wurfel 1988, 124).

When the Amnesty International mission visited detention centers in 1975 to interview prisoners, they concluded that there was "convincing evidence that the employment of torture was widespread" (Amnesty International 1976, 13). More serious than detention were the rising cases of disappearances and salvaging (extrajudicial execution). By the late 1970s, the number of detentions was dropping, but disappearances and "extrajudicial execution" were rising (Amnesty International 1982, 4): an estimated thirty annual disappearances and fifty salvagings occurred between 1976 and 1978 (Wurfel 1988, 126).

The Marcos regime did constrain mass political participation. It used referenda and controlled elections to depoliticize people and employed repression when such depoliticization was not successful. As we see below, Marcos installed his regime in such a way that he was able to give himself significantly expanded powers, compared with those that he possessed as a democratically elected president.

ILL-DEFINED EXECUTIVE POWER

The limits to the leader's—or leaders'—power are "formally ill-defined" (Linz 1964, 297). Constitutions are often changed or suspended, leaving unclear the exact powers that the leader has under the authoritarian regime. Such vagueness works to the leader's advantage because it allows him to give to himself more powers as needed. However, we can predict a general limit to the leader's power by identifying the members of his coalition, since in order to retain their support he will need to meet their interests.

In the Philippines, Marcos used constitutional procedures to expand his power. The declaration of martial law was legal under the 1935 constitution, which stated that such emergency powers could be implemented when the country was under threat of "invasion, insurrection, or rebellion" (Del Carmen 1979, 87). Once martial law was in effect, Marcos revised the draft of the 1973 constitution to widen his powers. Although the transitory provisions were written ostensibly to ensure a smooth transition from 1935 to the 1973 constitution, in practice they expanded the scope and strength of the president's power.

First, the provisions delegated to Marcos judicial and legislative powers and expanded his executive powers. Until Marcos constituted the interim National Assembly, he would in effect be the sole legislator, since Congress had been closed. Members of the judiciary, including the Supreme Court, and the bureaucracy had to submit undated letters of resignation to Marcos; thus, he was able to oust government officials by simply naming a successor (Del Carmen 1979, 91; Abueva 1979, 42–43). He also stipulated that until the interim National Assembly was constituted, he would rule under the powers accorded to the president under the 1935 constitution and to the prime minister under the 1973 constitution.

Second, he guaranteed the length of these powers by giving himself the power to implement the 1973 constitution at a rate that he decided. Until the 1973 constitution was fully operating, Marcos would continue to control judicial, legislative, and executive powers. Furthermore, all presidential decrees and orders would remain legal even after martial law ended (Abueva 1979, 38). In effect, then, not only were Marcos's powers virtually unlimited in scope, they were also unlimited across time.

The 1973 constitution was amended in 1976 and 1981, further expanding Marcos's powers. In 1976, Amendment 3 stipulated that even when the interim National Assembly was constituted, Marcos would continue to hold the powers of president under the 1935 constitution as well as those of prime minister under the 1973 constitution. Amendment 5 allowed Marcos to retain legislative powers until the end of martial law. Amendment 6 expanded his legislative powers to state that even if the regular National Assembly were constituted, Marcos could still legislate via executive order whenever he deemed that such action was necessary; furthermore, such legislation would automatically become binding (Cortes 1980, 23; Hernandez 1985a, 246).

While there were few constitutional limits on Marcos's power, and although the constitution was in fact used to increase his powers, Marcos did have some limits, determined by the interests of his support coalition. To the extent that their interests were met, he would remain in power; to the extent that their interests were not met, they would defect from the coalition.

At the beginning of martial law, Marcos's support coalition included the military, technocrats, big businessmen, friends and family of the Marcoses, the church, and the United States government (Abueva 1979, 55; Bello, Kinley, and Elinson 1982, 15–16; Hawes 1987, 14). Thus, the coalition favored conservative measures, such as political order and capitalist development, and did not favor mass-based politics (Hawes 1987, 52).

To create this coalition, Marcos distributed to its members resources or policies that would meet their interests. The military received significant increases in salaries and supplies. The technocrats were allowed to reorganize the bureaucracy to streamline policy implementation (Abueva 1979). Businessmen and friends and family of the Marcoses received financial favors, such as agricultural monopolies (Bello, Kinley, and Elinson 1982; Hawes 1987). The church received the continuation of such favorable policies as the ban on divorce and the nontaxation of church property. The United States government was allowed to maintain its military bases; furthermore, the Philippines promised to defeat the New People's Army.

However, in order to retain his authoritarian powers, Marcos had to maintain his support coalition. In this sense, there were predictable limits on Marcos's power. To the extent that his power was based on his coalition, he was not free to behave in a way that would threaten the interests of his coalition members and therefore cause them to defect from the coalition. Thus, since the coalition included members who wanted economic growth or wealth, Marcos had to propose an economic program that would produce enough resources to distribute across his coalition. Since the United States did not want Communist forces to increase in power, Marcos had to successfully contain them.

While the leader receives increased powers under authoritarianism, these powers arrive neither cost-free nor guaranteed to last. Concerning cost, if the leader cannot meet the interests of his entire support coalition, then he must rank order the coalition members and meet their interests accordingly. However, this process risks alienating the less valued members. In the Philippines, as the economic crisis grew after 1980, Marcos chose to meet the demands of his friends and family members over those of other businessmen. For example, he created a $630 million bailout fund to buoy the bankrupt businesses of his cronies (Bello, O'Connor, and Broad 1982, 190–91). While this move retained his cronies' support, it diminished the support of businessmen who were not cronies and therefore who were hurt by the cronies' ability to gain easy credits and guarantees. As a result, by the early 1980s, demonstrations against the Marcos regime became commonplace in Makati, the financial district of Metro-Manila.

Marcos did have ill-defined executive power. He implemented the 1935 and the 1973 constitutions as they benefited him, he had the constitutions amended to increase the scope of his power, and he had vast legislative powers through his use of executive decrees. To maintain support for his regime, he used these expanded powers not only to benefit himself but also to meet the interests of the members of his support coalition, particularly the First Family and its cronies.

CONCLUSION

There can be little question that the regime Marcos instituted in the Philippines in 1972 was authoritarian. It closed down political institutions such as Congress; it used as its rationale the threat of government overthrow by Communist insurgents and the opportunity for reform; it curtailed mass participation in politics; and it expanded Marcos's personal power. Furthermore, the installation of an authoritarian regime directly affected both the church and the military. The church became an avenue for political participation as traditional institutions, such as the legislature, were closed. The church was increasingly lobbied by the mass public to defend it from political repression. The military's power increased as the regime's basis for legitimacy called for the military to end the Communist insurgency. Furthermore, the military's role was expanded as it was used by Marcos to implement his orders. The next two chapters discuss in depth the effect authoritarianism had on the roles and activities of both the church and the military.

.

II

4 Marcos and the Church

INTRODUCTION

■ The Philippine Catholic church shifted its focus from a purely religious mission before authoritarianism, focusing on the sacraments and charity, to a more active and overtly political role under the Marcos regime. The impetus for this change was due to both internal and external factors. The church experienced internal pressure to change through the introduction of a new ideology by the Second Vatican Council, which encouraged the church to adopt an active role in socioeconomic reform. However, the church was also pressured externally by the authoritarian regime itself, which encouraged the institution to support the regime while simultaneously enacting policies that went against church precepts. This change in focus led to a widening schism between the bishops, who supported a more traditional stance, and the priests and nuns, who pushed for greater political intervention against the regime. Eventually, the bishops saw that the only way to reunify the church was to join the rank and file and adopt a political stance. Thus, conflict within the institution eventually led to its active work to oust the Marcos regime.

FROM RELIGIOUS MISSION TO VATICAN II

In the 1950s, the Philippine church was conservative, focusing on the spiritual rather than the material world (Shoesmith 1985,

73). The Philippine church defined its role as one of religious mission: to educate people and to administer sacraments. Of the thirty-four church informants interviewed for this book, most of them believed that the church initially took a position of nonintervention in socioeconomic or political issues, that it became involved in such issues slowly, and that even when it did transform its role, it was still mostly traditional in outlook. When asked what the church did once it became involved, six informants mentioned that the church tried to influence policy indirectly through the release of pastoral letters and statements by the Catholic Bishops' Conference of the Philippines (CBCP), and four mentioned farmers' organizations, including the Federation of Free Farmers (FFF).

One brother pointed out that the "church was not that active before martial law. It was powerful, but it wasn't using that power to get people together. It was complacent." Although the church realized the conditions of the poor, "its efforts were scattered" and were not focused on reform. Before Vatican II, it stressed its ecclesiastical role: teaching and attending to church ceremonies and sacraments. During the years immediately before martial law, the church began to see the need for societal change, especially economic reform. However, while it became aware of the condition of the poor, its efforts were mostly charitable, never confrontational, and mostly channeled through lay organizations such as Catholic Action. Since these organizations were closely tied to the church, they did not try to change socioeconomic conditions through influencing public policy or changing governments, but instead they focused on ameliorating human suffering on a case-by-case basis. As a result, church efforts during this period were characterized as "paternalistic and charitable" (Giordano 1988, 21).

In general, while the bishops accepted the Vatican II changes in principle, they did not aggressively implement them (Giordano 1988, 88). While Vatican II called for looking at the temporal side of the people of God and focusing on economic development needs, the CBCP warned that the church must always focus on its religious mission and not go off on a sociopolitical tangent (90). Although agreeing in principle with the concept of the church community as the people of God, the CBCP stressed their hierarchical superiority and their role as "the traditional idea of sanctifying and saving souls" (89). Thus, while acknowledging that Basic Christian Communities (BCCs) have church sanction, the CBCP encouraged neither lay participation in church rites nor the expansion of the BCC network (91).

The exceptions to the traditional passive position of the church were found in the work of Father Hogan in forming the Federation of Free Workers (FFW) and in laymen creating the Federation of Free Farmers (FFF). The Federation of Free Workers was formed in 1950 to actively work for "the living wage of the Filipino worker," through a specifically non-Communist, church-influenced organization (Fabros 1988, 38). In 1953, two laymen who had attended seminars at the church's Institute for Social Order created an organization (with similar methods and goals) for farmers, the Federation of Free Farmers, especially those who had initially supported the Hukbalahap movement (44–45). However, these groups were not representative of church work at that time, in that they organized people to lobby government for structural change rather than worked on an individual level to ameliorate short-term and small-scope needs.

The CBCP released seven pastoral letters from 1968 to 1972. Of these seven, four concerned the church's role as teacher and stressed the importance of strict hierarchical rule, one called for socioeconomic reform, and two addressed political issues. Of the four traditional letters, three stated the church's position on birth control, celibacy for the clergy, and drug use (Hardy 1984). In 1970, with the impending visit of Pope Paul X, the CBCP used the occasion to reiterate the hierarchical nature of the church by pointing out the line of command, from the pope to the bishops, from the bishops to the priests.

However, in the same year, the church began to shift its role to include socioeconomic and political issues, as the Vatican II ideology began to gain more adherents. Out of thirty-four church informants, eleven said that the church became involved in politics by the early 1970s. When asked why the church became involved then, informants offered a range of responses, from specific incidents that the church reacted against to more general reasons inherent in the church's self-image. One informant pointed to peasant and worker uprisings led by the Communist Party of the Philippines, which caused the clergy to take a countering response. Six mentioned stimuli from the church in Rome, where popes from the 1950s to Vatican II encouraged church involvement in social action and began to discuss liberation theology. Three informants who took a broader view of why the church became involved pointed to socioeconomic conditions in the Philippines in general, and in particular a church-sponsored conference in 1967 to discuss agrarian issues, the teaching of liberation theology in the Philippines, and the church's being lobbied by cause-oriented groups.

Seven informants believed that the church had always been involved in issues concerning the temporal world. One informant said that the church entered the political arena as early as 1957, to protest the elections, which were notorious for their level of electoral fraud. However, more informants saw the church's early political role as supporting rather than critiquing the government. They stated that the church's initial traditional role was actually political because, by not pressuring for change, it supported the government and legitimized government policies. One respondent said that the church has always been involved because it cannot "do [its] job without being involved in politics." Another informant stated, "Ever since the Spanish times, even during American times, the church has been involved. Then, the church was on the side of the Right. It defended institutional interests."

A call for socioeconomic reform was the theme for only one pastoral letter before martial law. The "Report of the Philippine Hierarchy to the People of God in the Philippines on their Deliberations at the Annual Bishops Conference," released in 1971, reiterated the responsibility of the laity to address poverty through such organizations as the FFW and FFF. On the other hand, the bishops accepted that they themselves must become involved in the solution, through the expansion of Basic Christian Communities and through allowing clergy and religious to share "more intimately in the Bishops' role of moral leadership" (Hardy 1984, 39).

Two pastoral letters were released in 1970 that overtly discussed political issues. The first one, "For a Non-Partisan Constitutional Convention," called for clean elections to select delegates to the Constitutional Convention (ConCon). It listed the corrupt electoral practices of past elections and said that it was a moral obligation to make sure that they did not recur. However, this letter again stressed that the bulk of the responsibility rested with the laity. The second pastoral letter released in 1970, the "Statement on Civic Responsibility," stressed that the bishops themselves "as Pastors of the people of God in this country, must speak out against these ills or be derelict in our duty" (Hardy 1984, 29). However, just as they had a moral obligation to speak out, so too did the mass public have a moral obligation to "conscientiously participate in the political life of the country," that is, to vote (30).

As the church began to change its role from religious mission to Vatican II teachings, as shown by the thematic shift of pastoral letters during this time period, the institution began to fragment and become conflicted. A schism emerged between traditional members, who wanted the institution to remain conservative and noninterventionist, and Vatican II supporters, who wanted the church to enter the temporal world and actively work for economic and political justice. A Jesuit priest stated that initial frustration with the church's predominantly traditional activities caused the institution to fragment.

Many of the people who joined these groups [in the 1960s] became frustrated and joined the extreme Left/Communist groups. Because, first, [there was a] lack of support by the church hierarchy and laity for reform. Only the Communists were for social transformation. Then, the only choices were Right and Left. Second, [there was the] perception that without the coming to power of the Communists, there would be no social transformation . . . . Third, spiritually, pre–Vatican II, the church was rigid. It had shallow intellectual roots. Vatican II was the coup de grace to ailing spirituality. (At that time, the Church could not give a synthesis to solve social promises.) Marx looked like it had the synthesis. Marx became the replacement for a Thomist or neo-Thomist world view.

As a result, he said, the church fragmented into three camps. The first camp, the largest segment of the church, tried to resist change. They were "apathetic [and] apolitical." Until the Aquino assassination occurred in 1983, they were not willing to make sacrifices or take risks for social change. The second camp wanted to create a "Third Force" between Marcos and the Communists. However, this group believed that while social change should be worked for, it should be done through lay groups, such as the Christian Democrats. The third camp was the Left, which used Marxism, particularly its historical materialism and theory of revolution, to analyze the socioeconomic condition and work for change.

Part of this fragmentation was due to the internal organization of the institutional church, with the bishops forming one group and the priests and nuns another. The Philippine church consists of approximately 100 bishops, 4,500 priests, 7,000 religious sisters, and 450 brothers. One-third of the priests are foreign missionaries, although most of the bishops and almost 80 percent of the sisters are Filipino (Giordano 1988, 12). The bishops, organized under the CBCP, ideologically espoused a position closest to Rome (Youngblood 1982, 31). This result is due to both generational and organizational factors. Most bishops were ordained prior to Vatican II. Also, the CBCP in the past has rewarded conservatism with promotions as a way to assure the least amount of ideological change within the institution itself (1982, 50–51).

However, the Association of Major Religious Superiors of the Philippines (AMRSP) actively carried out the prophetic role of the church. They took a strong position on socioeconomic issues by giving witness, that is, by living with the poor. In 1971, the AMRSP called for a restructuring of Philippine society in order to alleviate socioeconomic and political ills (Giordano 1988, 215). It was the first church organization to adopt a political role, stressing the need to protect human rights even in 1971, before the implementation of martial law (1988, 167).

This fragmentation was compounded by cleavages across organizations, as individual bishops, priests, and nuns pushed the church to expand its role. A group of bishops emerged that argued that the gains the socioeconomic lay groups had made would not remain without a corresponding change in the distribution of political power (Giordano 1988, 24). Bishops who were more liberation-oriented stressed the idea of the church as the people of God, while those who were more conservative were hesitant to embrace the idea of the church as a community rather than an institution (92–93). There were also extreme differences regarding just what political change entailed. New groups, both religious and lay, emerged. On the moderate side were the Christian Socialists (under Senator Raul Manglapus). On the more radical side were the Christians for National Liberation (under Father Edicio de la Torre) and individual priests and religious who sided with the National Democratic Front (23–24).

Thus, by the early 1970s, the church in the Philippines had slowly begun to transform its role from conservatism to sociopolitical action. On the one hand, the bishops clearly viewed their pastoral role to include speaking out against the political ills of the country. They stated that they themselves would be remiss if they did not accept their role to witness in the world. However, they believed that such action lay mostly in the realm of the laity. While it was the bishops' role to identify problems and offer solutions, it was the moral obligation of the laity to act, such as by voting, to redress such ills.

THE IMPACT OF AUTHORITARIANISM
ON THE CHURCH

When martial law was declared in 1972, the church took a more direct socioeconomic stand. In general, it was easier for the church to act in the economic development area because the Gospel could easily be applied to it. However, the church was afraid that if it addressed the political side of social injustice, it would become identified with a particular political party or actor (Giordano 1988, 3). After the declaration of martial law in 1972, though, the church increasingly felt forced to take a more direct political role. It saw its political choice as confined to two extremes: a regime led by the Communists or by Marcos. Thus, the church decided initially that it was wisest to support Marcos, even if it did not agree with martial law. It was only in 1977 that the institution specifically attacked the martial law regime (141). Only by 1979 did Cardinal Sin ask Marcos to step down and call for elections (147).

The informants' responses mirror this trend in the church of expanding its role from traditional to socioeconomic and political concerns, due to pressure from groups within the institution as well as from the Marcos regime itself. When asked to identify when the church became involved in political issues, eight pointed to the declaration of martial law. When asked why the church, or they personally, became politically involved, those who said that the church entered early also mentioned specifically political reasons for such involvement: the 1974 raid on the Sacred Heart novitiate, the regime's human rights violations, and the suppression of political rights. Two informants mentioned that the church's concern over socioeconomic conditions, especially its witnessing with the poor and identifying with their struggle, led the church to become involved in political issues. One sister said that she personally became involved in 1974 when she joined the Justice and Peace Commission of the AMRSP; before that experience, she said, "my world was very small."

Looking at the pastoral letters issued by the CBCP from 1973 through 1977, we can see this trend of the church moving away from focusing on teaching and hierarchy and toward socioeconomic and political conditions. We can also see from the letters the widening schism in the church as the bishops in this period try to be conciliatory, simultaneously taking both traditional and progressive positions. Of the eleven letters released during this period, five concern teaching and hierarchy, three are socioeconomic, and one is political. There are also two hybrid letters, both released in 1977, which mix a traditional and a political focus.

The five purely traditional letters were released in 1973, 1974, and 1976. Four of the letters focused on the role of the church as teacher, underscoring the church's position on such issues as birth control, abortion, marriage, and divorce (Hardy 1984). One letter stressed the need for strict obedience to hierarchy within the church. The pastoral letter, "To the Priests of the Philippines," first pointed out the correct role of a priest: "The central work of the priesthood of Jesus Christ is the work of religion—bringing God's word and His Sacraments to man and reconciling man to God. This must in every case remain the primary emphasis of our work" (Hardy 1984, 46).

Second, it reminded the priests that they are an extension of the immediate bishops under which they serve. Thus, they must obey not only bishops in general but the policy positions of their specific bishop (Hardy 1984, 44–51).

The three purely socioeconomic letters were released in 1973 and 1975 and called for people to analyze the conditions of injustice in the country and to try to alleviate them, using Lent and the International Year of Women as opportunities for such reflection (Hardy 1984). One letter, "On Evangelization and Development," pointed out the problems of underdevelopment in the Philippines (52–77). It stressed that the laity cannot follow the traditional solution of charity work, which appeases the upper and middle classes' feelings of guilt but does not solve poverty (59). Instead, the bishops argued that people must focus not on solving poverty on a case-by-case basis but by attacking the roots of the problem.

Because of the uneven level of development within the Philippines,

the hierarchy of the Philippines feels obligated to condemn the collective sin of unjust and anachronistic structures—not as if the church were some innocent outside observer but fully acknowledging her own share of responsibility. She must be courageous enough to admit her solidarity with the past, and to acknowledge her responsibility to the present and the future. (Hardy 1984, 60)

In this way, the letter links the church's role of evangelization to socioeconomic development.

In the midst of this apparent confusion it is important to stress that the Church has the prophetic task of awakening the conscience of the public, especially of those who are the decision-makers, in the light of God's demand for justice. The Church has received from Christ the mission of preaching the Gospel message, which contains a call to man to turn away from sin to the love of the Father, universal brotherhood and a consequent demand for justice in the world. (Hardy 1984, 65)

However, it is clear that while the letter calls for action, the church believes that the laity are the ones to take on a political role, acting according to their Catholic faith: "The Church's place . . . is not to direct this task, since it is a properly temporal task that falls within the competence of civil authority and societal institutions" (Hardy 1984, 69–70).

The official position of the CBCP, up to the late 1970s, was that of "critical collaboration" (Giordano 1988, 184). It portrayed itself as neither pro- nor anti-Marcos. Cardinal Sin took a position of negotiation and conciliation with the regime. Sin spoke out early on, criticizing the military's human rights abuses, the regime's suspension of political rights, and the lack of land reform. He called on the regime to increase participation and to "normalize" martial law (Stockwin 1974a, 16–17). However, he was moderate in his approach so as not to antagonize the regime, thereby protecting the church's institutional interests. Thus, Sin and Marcos agreed on a policy of "mutual collaboration" (Stockwin 1974b, 14). One example of this attempt to cooperate was the formation of the Church-Military Liaison Committee (CMLC), created to resolve differences between the two sides, especially concerning the detention of priests and religious workers (Youngblood 1978, 517). However, the regime viewed this committee as a way to institutionalize church support for, if not complicity with, its policies; as a result, it did not feel bound to keep CMLC agreements and in fact ignored many of them.

Thus, the CBCP asked people to cooperate with the regime by voting in referenda and elections even though they served not as representational processes but legitimizing ones (Giordano 1988, 143). Concerning human rights, it took stronger stands against population control and abortion than against the torture of political prisoners (144). The CBCP admitted that people must be free to follow their conscience, even on the question of using violence. However, the thrust of the CBCP's position was that the church should take a moral role and leave politics to the lay community (186). It argued that if the church were to carry out a political role, it would cause public confusion and thus worsen the political situation (188).

While the bishops tried to encourage the laity to work for social justice, individual bishops and the rank and file within the institution adopted a socioeconomic role early on. Bishops and religious on the island of Mindanao were some of the first to take a stand against martial law. In 1972, all of the bishops and the heads of religious orders and lay organizations of Mindanao drafted a letter to be read from the pulpit attacking the regime's economic policies, the climate of fear regarding labor organizing, the lack of freedom of speech and the press, family planning, the treatment of detainees, and the signs of martial law rule being consolidated (A Plea From the Pulpit 1974, 22–23). The AMRSP took a strong position arguing that they must adapt themselves to the lives of the people (Giordano 1988, 118). In

1973, the Jesuit provincial declared "that witnessing to justice and service of the poor was the primary task of the Society of Jesus in the Philippines" (25).

Because the CBCP insisted on holding on to traditional roles, even in the face of Vatican II changes and in the emergence of an authoritarian regime in the Philippines, several bishops began to openly break away from the official position. Seventeen bishops signed a statement, "Ut Omnes Unum Sint" ("That all may be one"), which called for the church to take a strong prophetic role: "We cannot conceive of a Church that preaches a Gospel which has nothing whatsoever to tell people in the political aspects of their life" (Giordano 1988, 144). They argued that the role of witnessing included not only the socioeconomic condition of the poor but the political condition of the oppressed. Thus, they called for the church to take an overtly opposition stand against the Marcos regime. They strengthened their position by pointing out "that the less involved in politics the Church professes to be, the more it is actually involved, but in a way that is most detrimental to its primary task of preaching the Gospel. For silence can mean condoning political "oppression" (187).

The rank and file, in general, tried to pressure the church as an institution to adopt a direct political role soon after martial law was implemented. The Association of Major Religious Superiors in the Philippines (AMRSP) argued that "the imposition of martial law had given rise to certain moral issues which the Church must address and could not avoid without the charge of being unfaithful to her Christian vocation" (Giordano 1988, 63). It also spoke up against the regime's repression of church groups and the deportation of foreign missionaries. It complained about the distortion of news in the regime-controlled media and established rival newspapers, newsletters, and radio stations (170–71). It also followed up such stands with action, creating task forces to deal with such issues as human rights abuses; it encouraged members to live with the poor; and it accepted political action as a viable route to liberation (64). By the mid-1970s, the more radical church members were turning to Latin America for ideology and models of action. A few priests took as their role model the Colombian priest Camilo Torres, who joined the Communist forces in the mountains, becoming a priest-guerrilla and eventually being killed in warfare (Wideman 1976, 27).

Role differences between conservative and progressive members of the church became pointed in 1975, when a plebiscite was scheduled to vote on whether or not people supported martial law. The CBCP supported voting, while the AMRSP opposed it and called for a boycott. The apostolic nuncio, transmitting Rome's fear of an open break between the two organizations, asked the AMRSP to follow the hierarchy for the sake of unity. "The Nuncio made it clear he considered the referendum a political act, not a moral issue or a matter of individual conscience" (Ocampo 1981a, 17). A group of moderate bishops asked Marcos to end martial law and proclaimed that they would boycott the referendum (Giordano 1988, 168). Bishop Claver complained that Rome's position seemed to be that when "a churchman praises martial law as good, that is not politics. When another churchman criticises martial law as subversive of human rights, that is politics" (Ocampo 1981a, 17).

The political letter, "Statement on the Referendum of February 27, 1975," listed safeguards necessary for the referendum to be free and meaningful (Hardy 1984, 127–29). It also stated that those who truly believe that no referendum can be free under martial law are free to follow their own consciences and not vote, even though it may go against the views of other people (128). Thus, on the one hand the CBCP wanted people to vote and was pressuring the regime to institute reforms to encourage voter turnout, but on the other hand it did not want to make voting a mandatory moral act.

The increasing fragmentation within the CBCP into conservative, moderate, and radical groups became even more pronounced in the mid-1970s, as these groups began to release their own statements independent of the CBCP organization. In 1976, for another referendum, twelve bishops and ten major religious superiors signed a statement informing the head of the CBCP that they were forced to act according to their own consciences rather than follow the prescribed activity of voting (Giordano 1988, 147–48). While the seventeen bishops signed "Ut Omnes Unum Sint," which proposed a liberation thrust to evangelization, two bishops countered by releasing their own statement, "Et Veritas Liberabit Vos" ("And the truth shall set you free"), which proposed a more cautious, development-oriented role for the church (47). Also in 1976, a position paper was discussed by a group of Jesuit provincial superiors, outlining the range of overtly political positions that the church could take: supporting the martial law regime, adopting constructive criticism, adopting peaceful opposition, or supporting a group on the revolutionary Left (215).

As church activity became increasingly political, the regime began to openly attack it for "interfering" in politics. It spread rumors that the church was actually trying to build a radical Christian political party (Wideman 1976, 26). More seriously, the regime tried to capitalize on the growing fragmentation within the church by saying that the "Christian left" was harming the church's institutional interests under martial law. The regime also took strong direct action against the church. It tried to diminish foreign influence, which tended to be more progressive, by limiting visas for foreign priests from five years to one year (Tasker 1976a, 11). In 1976, the regime closed two religious publications, *Signs of the Times* and *The Communicator,* and two church-run radio stations, claiming that church ownership was not a "license to undermine the work of the Government, to subvert the security of the republic, or to incite people into action against public authority" (Tasker 1976b, 14–15; Youngblood 1990, 114–25). The regime also arrested Catholic workers in Mindanao and expelled two American missionaries.

The initial reaction of the church hierarchy to the regime's harassment was subdued. To ensure that the church did not antagonize the regime and therefore risk harming its institutional interests, the pope sent a letter to the CBCP calling for restraint and for a strict hierarchical line of command (Tasker 1976a, 12). Cardinal Sin tried to straddle the issue, to appease Rome, Marcos, and the progressive church. On the one hand, he downplayed the regime's charges of a leftist church, saying that he did not "believe that there is such a thing as a leftist Christian, because if you are a leftist you are a communist and therefore you are not a Christian" (10). On the other hand, he pronounced that the church would not intervene in political affairs. "I have said that as a Church and as churchmen we are not really concerned about the form of government—it could be a dictatorship . . . or democracy" (10–11). However, he also stated that the church's primary concern was to end violence. Bishop Claver stated that the church should repudiate neither the NPA nor the regime. "The question we ask with regard to the two political extremes is simply this: to what extent are they working for the genuine good of the people?" (12).

The two hybrid letters were released in 1977. The first pastoral letter, "To Our People: The Bond of Love in Proclaiming the Good News," asked the regime to reconsider its position of repressing evangelical workers and foreign missionaries (Hardy 1984, 145–48).

Throughout her whole history, the Church has always upheld the right of the State to protect itself against any threat to its existence. This we have never doubted. The Church has likewise upheld the Gospel to all men at all times. This right deriving from the Divine Command has been generally respected by all Nations. Our own Nation bears that salient distinction. But like other God-given rights this right should not be denied in the case of National Security. (Hardy 1984, 147)

The bishops surprised Marcos, and themselves, by uniting right and left positions in the CBCP annual conference to produce this pastoral letter. The CBCP felt that it was important for the church to offer a united front to show the regime that it could not be fragmented and to strengthen the CBCP's message attacking martial law (Tasker 1977, 20). It also wanted to dispel any suspicions that the Vatican had given the Marcos regime "Its tacit assurance that it will not interfere in any crackdown on what it clearly considers to be undesirable elements in the Philippine Church" (22).

The second letter, "Position Paper on the Synod Theme Catechetics in Our Time with Special Reference to Catechetics for Children and Adults," offered the first reference that authoritarianism should not be supported (Hardy 1984, 149–64). While repeating the church's position on such issues as abortion and contraception, it added that in "today's world one needs more than mere teaching in words about Christ and His message. One needs environs which live the message of reconciliation and sharing as brought to us by Christ" (151). Thus, church teaching should be used "to re-examine not only the culture and economic structure of the country, but also the political context within which the Church is called upon to unfold her message," particularly given the authoritarian nature of the government (156).

It is noted with grave concern that political issues are beginning to create divisions within the ranks of the clergy and the faithful. There is even a tendency to approve of the system of authoritarianism, regardless of the adverse effects to human religious liberty which it may entail. There is also a growing rift—a chasm of mutual indifference—between those who seek to assert, at least implicitly, the primacy of liberation from material wants and those who rightly insist that the Church's primary mission is the proclamation of the Good News to all men. (Hardy 1984, 156)

Thus, the church was fragmenting horizontally, within the organizations, and vertically, between them. Liberation-oriented bishops sided with the AMRSP against the tradition-oriented bishops (Giordano 1988, 121). The tension between the superiors and the bishops was reflected in the polarization of AMRSP members, in the mid-1970s, to the point where some superiors refused to attend organizational meetings (118). To avoid an open breach between the two organizations, the AMRSP left open the possibility of conciliation with the bishops by saying that dialogue was needed not only between the church and the people but also within the church itself, across the different organizational and hierarchical levels (118). However, even when conflict occurred between superiors and bishops, or between the AMRSP and the CBCP, the former agreed to follow the leadership of the hierarchy while at the same time underlining their commitment to the social mission (120–21).

CONFLICT AND CHANGE WITHIN THE CHURCH

By the late 1970s, the church's cautious political position slowly changed. As the institution's role moved from socioeconomic to political concerns, the level of conflict within the institution rose significantly. Thus, from 1978 to 1983, the schism in the church began to widen: the conservatives wanted the church to continue to focus on its religious mission and to protect hierarchical control; the moderates agreed that the Vatican II reforms must be implemented; and the radicals were pressuring the church not only to take a direct role in socioeconomic reform but also to actively oppose the Marcos regime.

Four informants said either that the church as an institution or they personally became politically involved during the late 1970s. Of those who dated the church's involvement from 1978 to 1983, all four mentioned political reasons as the stimuli. Two said that, after a while, church members could no longer give the regime the benefit of the doubt. One religious brother said that a "few years after martial law, when changes hadn't occurred still, that's when more and more church people [got] dissatisfied with the administration and started involving themselves." A lay worker agreed, stating that at

the individual level, bishops began fighting the government and the military in 1972. But at the national level, when it was really noticeable, was in the midseventies when martial law began to sour in everyone's eyes. The church became an actor on the national scene, not a consistent actor, but a major one. . . . When martial law began, the bishops said that it was not all bad. They were willing to give martial law a chance. They said maybe it's a good thing. But by the midseventies, it was clear that martial law was not the answer. There was a buildup in the church. More and more people were becoming ideologically involved and critical. The bishops began to respond to pressure from below.

Looking at the pastoral letters released from the CBCP during this time period, we can see the widening break within the institution. Of the eight letters released, five concern traditional teaching and hierarchy issues. The other three letters are hybrids: two discuss both tradition and socioeconomic conditions, while one discusses socioeconomic conditions and political concerns. Thus, on the one hand, the conservative members are trying to keep the institution on the right, focusing on its religious mission and noninvolvement in politics. However, the more progressive members were beginning to try to pull the church more to the left, and were taking more political and less conciliatory positions.

The traditional letters were released in 1978, 1980, and 1982. The first pastoral letter, "On the Holy Father," reasserted the primacy of the word of the pope and mentioned the elevation in power of the bishops with the creation of the synod, thus arguing for strict hierarchical control (Hardy 1984, 165–72). Three letters released in 1980 discussed the primacy of religious teaching, hierarchical obedience, and the beatification of Lorenzo Ruiz, a Filipino martyr. In 1982, the pastoral letter, "A Church Sent," reminded the faithful that the pope, on his visit the previous year, gave the Philippines the special task of spearheading missionary work in Asia (227–31).

The two hybrid letters that discuss tradition and socioeconomic conditions were released in 1978 and 1979. In 1978, the pastoral letter, "Education for Justice," was actually far reaching in its calls for change. While it repeated traditional values, it also called for socioeconomic reform and admitted that the church itself, as an institution, might need to be reformed. The letter severely criticized the economic development path the Philippines had taken because it had not respected human life (Hardy 1984, 173–200). It stated that parochial schools and the right to life should be protected. However, it went on to demand that all sectors of society work for reform. It called on the regime to implement political equality for all social groups (178). It called on the mass public as a whole to accept its responsibility for the socioeconomic conditions of the country (179). While it reminded people to work for reform, it stressed that injustice, suffering, and oppression do not justify the use of violence to solve the social condition (175). Finally, the CBCP admitted that it also has a role to play. "The Church is fully aware that if she is to be credible in her preaching of justice, she should precede all others in the living example of a just institution, just in her word, in her sacraments and in her pastoral action" (177).

The second tradition–socioeconomic conditions hybrid, the pastoral letter, "On the Life of the Unborn Child: 'Thou Shalt Not Kill,' " was released to celebrate the fact that the United Nations declared 1979 the International Year of the Child (Hardy 1984, 201–06). In this letter, the bishops shifted the traditional message of respect for life to include not only fetuses but also society as a whole. Thus, while attacking the use of contraceptives and the practice of prostitution, it also condemned violence (including kidnappings and the forcible ejection of the poor and the powerless) and discrimination (because it created the impression that some lives are more valuable than others).

In the one socioeconomic conditions and politics hybrid, the pastoral letter, "Exhortation Against Violence," the bishops attacked the escalation of violence and changed their opinion, stating that it is not forbidden for people to use violence in certain circumstances (Hardy 1984, 207–12). They pointed to poverty as the cause of this escalation and admitted that because of destitution, moral people were turning to violence. They spoke

not only of the radical and impatient revolutionaries who have already taken up arms and are even now engaged in intensifying guerrilla warfare, but also of many committed Christians, especially younger ones, who in growing numbers, believe that the very exigencies of their faith and their sense of justice commit them to solidarity with, and action for the victims of social, economic and political injustices. (Hardy 1984, 209)

Thus, they felt compelled to admit that they could not judge people who use violence as a way to follow their consciences (Hardy 1984, 209). But they called for an end to the escalation of violence in Philippine society and repeated the words of Pope John Paul II, that "whatever are the miseries and sufferings of men, *it will never be through violence*, power play or political systems, but through the truth about men that mankind will find its way to a better future" (211).

After the 1978 elections, when charges arose of electoral impropriety ensuring the election of the Marcoses, among other KBL candidates, the CBCP was deeply split over what its position should be. Eventually, the moderate position won out. Rather than antagonizing the regime, the CBCP laid the blame partially at the feet of the voters themselves (Ocampo 1978a, 24). As a conciliatory gesture, Sin, in an open letter to the faithful, asked them to send him accounts of electoral cheating, which he then turned over to United States Vice President Walter Mondale, who was touring Southeast Asia (The Wrath of Cardinal Sin 1978, 35).

Sin found himself increasingly caught between the progressive group of bishops, which wanted the church to have a presence in the "people's political and economic struggles," and the more conservative group, which wanted to remain out of politics

(Ocampo 1978a, 24). Sin himself feared that church involvement in political issues would trigger a period of neoclericalism. Marcos was able to successfully drive a wedge between the conservative and progressive bishops by playing on the former's fears of the loss of those privileges that the government had traditionally accorded the church, such as the tax-exempt status of church property and the refusal to confiscate and redistribute church real estate (24). In 1978, the IBP (interim National Assembly) introduced two bills, on population control and divorce, which, although they had little chance in passing, were again meant as examples of how the regime could harm the church's institutional interests (Ocampo 1978b, 17; Youngblood 1978, 516).

The division within the church began to further fragment, in 1979, as the Left broke into two antagonistic camps and began to organize the laity. The two groups, the National Democrats (Nat-Dems) and the Socialist Democrats (Soc-Dems) both opposed the Marcos regime. The National Democrats evolved out of pre–martial law reformist groups, such as the FFF. They called for fundamental structural change in society but also wanted change within the church, to make it more nationalist and democratic. They did not create an overarching organization but rather formed an alliance with existing mass organizations revolving around the urban poor, youth, and religious men and women (Ocampo 1979, 33; Wurfel 1988, 217). The Socialist Democrats saw themselves as a third force, in the same vein as European Christian Democratic parties. They evolved out of such 1960s organizations as the Christian Social Movement. While they were against the martial law regime, they were also against the radicalism of the National Democrats. They took a moderate position in their opposition and allied with traditional political opposition members. They did not call for an institutional restructuring of the church, in large part because they depended heavily on the church's grassroots organization as their base, but they did call for the expulsion of Marxists among the religious rank and file.

They created their own political group, the United Democratic Socialist Party of the Philippines (NPDSP) (Ocampo 1979, 33; Wurfel 1988, 218; Youngblood 1990, 82).

By 1979, hostilities between the regime and the church had also intensified. Defense Minister Enrile charged that "religious radicals" in the countryside were spreading anti-Marcos propaganda and were encouraging people to support the New People's Army. Sin defended the church members' activities, saying that "if priests were involved in the people's problems, it was at least partly because many Filipinos believed they could not receive just or fair treatment from the martial-law government" (Vokey 1979, 28–29). He reiterated, though, that even in this situation, the role of a priest is very different from that of a politician because the priest espouses no particular ideology and does not want political power for himself. Sin argued that, by helping people with their political grievances, priests were fulfilling their religious mission (28). "When people lose faith in their leaders, fear the military and don't trust the courts the only person left for them to go to with their grievances is their parish priest . . . and [the priest] cannot just file away their complaints like everyone else and pretend they do not exist. He has to act, to do something, or he too will lose all hope" (Church Militant 1979, 67).

The regime's attack against the church caused Sin to shift his position closer to the Left. While still not taking for himself the position of the more radical members of the church, he nevertheless defended them. He did shift his position on human rights violations, stating that it was the duty of the church to speak out against such abuse (Vokey 1979, 29). However, this shift in Sin's position did not satisfy the Left. Leftists pushed for him to speak out against the martial law regime itself, and not just its side effects, arguing that his silence connoted support. Thus, in 1979, Sin called for Marcos to step down, warning that continuation of martial law would further erode the social condition and cause a revolution (Church Militant 1979, 58).

The split within the CBCP and AMRSP became more pronounced by the early 1980s. Within the CBCP, a moderate group of nine bishops emerged in 1980 to try to bridge this widening break. On the one hand, they agreed with the more critical view of the Marcos regime and took a position against martial law. On the other hand, they refused to join with the group of radical bishops; instead, they denounced the use of violence against the regime (Giordano 1988, 189). A similar split was beginning to be more obvious in the AMRSP, although the AMRSP took a much more progressive position than the CBCP. In 1979, the AMRSP decided to discuss the issue of evangelization and political involvement brought up at Puebla. In 1981, the chairman of the AMRSP stated that the plebiscite "was an immoral manipulation of the people to suit the political ambitions of a few and was a violation of the constitution" (169).

Seeing that pressure placed on Sin was causing the opposite of what he wanted, Marcos tried to use the 1981 papal visit to legitimize his regime (implying that the pope would only visit the Philippines if he approved of martial law) and to place hierarchical pressure on the church to pull out of politics (Saints and Sinners 1981, 34). The pope, while taking a position to the right of Sin, chastised the regime. He attacked Marcos's human rights record and abuse of power and told Marcos that "a nation's security interests should not be allowed to take precedence over the people's human rights and dignity" (Tasker and Ocampo 1981, 8). However, the pope also reiterated a strict hierarchical line of command and told priests to focus on their role as moral teachers.

By the late 1970s and early 1980s, the Left made up between 10 and 20 percent of the bishops (Ocampo 1981a, 16; Wurfel 1988, 216). However, the Left had been successful in creating a parallel organization that threatened both the institution and the regime. The institutional church was ignored as attention shifted to a church of the people, or grassroots church, created by the Left through the expansion of BCCs. Whereas the institutional church reiterated hierarchical traditions, the grassroots approach decentralized structures and traditions, focusing instead on the people of God. The institutional church began to fear that leftists might use the church of the people as an organizational base of armed revolt (Ocampo 1981a, 17). By 1983, the original seventeen bishops protested the increasing militarization of society and called for the church to act at the local levels, through BCCs. As a conciliatory gesture, they added that such BCC "involvement cannot be the same as that of a political party" (Giordano 1988, 190).

The regime also felt threatened by the grassroots church. The church of the people had begun to eat away at the legitimacy of local political leaders by offering parallel social programs (Ocampo 1981a, 17). "In the absence of a real political process, the communities often offer the only non-violent channel for protest" (Leftward Christian Soldiers? 1982, 58). The BCCs were becoming so numerous that their potential power to erode the regime could no longer be ignored. However, while Marcos felt threatened by the BCCs, he was afraid to openly attack the BCCs and risk unifying the church, thereby assuring active Catholic opposition en masse to his regime.

Thus, in 1982, for different reasons, both the church hierarchy and the regime began to move against the leftist members of the church. In a meeting between the church and the military, of the Church-Military Liaison Committee, Defense Minister Enrile charged that the church was being infiltrated by Communist members (Ocampo 1982b, 38). The hierarchy's response was conciliatory. They felt that quick change was needed, to protect the institutional church. Thus, they began to quietly replace leftist members, especially those involved in social work and human rights work, with more conservative members (Ocampo 1982a, 31).

CHURCH OPPOSITION TO THE MARCOS REGIME

It was not until 1983 that the church accepted a role of direct political action, organizing opposition and working for the end of martial law. From 1983 to 1985, events began to escalate quickly within the church and between the church and the regime. The prime impetus for this escalation was the assassination of Senator Benigno Aquino at the Manila International Airport on August 21, 1983, while under the custody of a military escort. After this event, it became harder for the conservatives to take a conciliatory stand, and the way was open for the moderates and leftists to influence the church's role. Thus, we see the church after 1983 taking more of an open, aggressive position against the regime, not only criticizing it but also calling for its overthrow.

Of the four informants who dated the church's political involvement at 1983 or later, three of them said that it was due to the Aquino assassination. As one Sacred Heart sister said, "[Before] 1983, the choice was focused on either the Communists or Marcos. There was no middle point. Ninoy's death was a clear focal point for rallying." Two informants, one who pegged the involvement as after 1983 and one who could not set a particular year, mentioned involvement as a direct part of the church's moral role. One bishop stressed that there "are moral issues in political issues." One leftist priest said that "at first, there were only a few bishops, priests, and nuns who criticized Marcos. But when many injustices happened, then the church by its mandate must get involved." A religious superior complained that the military labeled "us as Communists. But we had to speak out because of the immorality of martial law." As one brother said, "Personally, there's a lot of difference. Before, I didn't care what happened, now I'm very much aware of what's happening. Before the Aquino assassination, the church people contented themselves in writing; after the assassination, they joined rallies, involved themselves with socioeconomic projects, and even educated the people on what's happening."

The pastoral letters that the CBCP released from 1983 to 1986 point out the struggle the organization was going through. The church was being forced to address the question of political involvement, because of the critical economic and political conditions caused by the economic crisis of the early 1980s. More and more, bishops realized that they could not even fulfill the cautious role of development without addressing political issues. Concerning the prophetic role, the CBCP also realized that concern for human rights abuses was not addressing the root problem. It came to the realization that two "critical and complex questions must also be faced: the questions of political involvement and the use of violence in the process of social transformation" (Giordano 1988, 179).

Three pastoral letters were released in 1983. The first letter was a socioeconomic and political hybrid; the last two letters were purely political. The first pastoral letter, "A Dialogue for Peace," was released after the CBCP decided to withdraw from the Church-Military Liaison Committee (Ocampo-Kalfors 1983, 10). It was one of the few such hybrids that pointedly analyzed the situations as being connected: that the economic and the political injustices fed on each other. It criticized the regime for choosing economic development programs, such as the attraction of investment from multinational corporations and the focus on tourism, that further eroded the position of the poor rather than aided in economic growth (Hardy 1984, 234). Thus, the letter signaled that the church was going to take a stronger position against the regime.

The letter argued that it was natural for people to link the regime's economic and political policies, since both of them created social injustice. Thus, the regime should not be surprised to see an increase of opposition against its rule (Hardy 1984, 234). Furthermore, it should not treat legitimate dissent as acts of subversion. "Insurgency—counter-militarization—is the response of segments of Philippine society that despair of any possibility of righting such wrongs" (235). Finally, the letter pointedly stated that political issues were the concern of the church because development and dissent are related to the church's mission of seeking justice (235). It restated the church's opposition to the detention of religious workers but also argued that such complaints no longer go far enough in fulfilling the church's role. Rather, it announced that the church would play a more aggressive role in taking a preferential option for the poor, but it would do so in a way that was ideologically neutral and did not lead to violence.

Hence, we will have to reprobate any action or program that runs counter to the primary values of the Gospel: the torture and murder of citizens simply because they are of a different political persuasion from that of present or would-be power holders; the silencing of people, the suppression of media merely because they speak the truth about our national situation; the increasing use of arms and violence by forces both on the right and on the left in the pursuit of their ends of power; and closer to home, the use of Church funds, the manipulation of Church programs, for the political purposes of ideological groups. (Hardy 1984, 235)

The second letter to be released in 1983, the "Message to the People of God," argued for the withdrawal of the Presidential Commitment Order, which authorized arrests without release on bail for national security reasons (Hardy 1984, 239). The bishops pointed out that this type of order went against the call they made in "A Dialogue for Peace" for regime tolerance of dissent as a legitimate form of political participation. Furthermore, this letter reiterated the economic and political problems mentioned in the earlier letter, stating that the regime had yet to act on them. Finally, it again complained of the politicization of the church from both the Right and the Left and called for a day of prayer in the country to "offer reparation to the Lord for all violations of human rights committed both [by] the Right and the Left" (240).

The third letter, the "Statement on Reconciliation Today," was released after the Aquino assassination. It warned that the condition of the country had become worse and that reconciliation was needed more than ever (Hardy 1984, 241–44).

Many events have pushed our country closer to the brink of chaos and anarchy. Among these events are numerous unexplained killings, the heinous crime of assassination at the Manila International Airport, the worsening economic insecurities brought by the inflation and devaluation, the widespread clamor for justice dramatized by all sectors of our society through rallies, demonstrations and strikes. (Hardy 1984, 241)

To address such problems, the letter listed political reforms that should be implemented immediately: the respect of human and political rights, freedom to dissent, a return to the values of "justice, truth, freedom and love," an end to election irregularities, a return of the military's loyalty to the Filipino people, and the end of violence from revolutionaries (Hardy 1984, 242–43).

After the Aquino assassination, Sin's position became more blatantly political and anti-Marcos. Referring to the Aquino assassination, Sin said that it "is the beginning, when people will be opening their eyes." He warned people not to underestimate the political power of the church. Its "role as a galvanizing force behind those in sympathy with the principles symbolised by Aquino's death is becoming a major political factor with which Marcos will have to contend" (Sacerdoti 1983, 18). However, Sin still argued that the work must be primarily carried out by laymen and that all action, while increasing the pressure on Marcos to return the country to democracy, must be nonviolent.

The church simultaneously tried to hold the different positions together, not wanting to alienate either side. Thus, while there seemed to be agreement that neither the Marcos regime nor a Communist government was acceptable, there was no sense of what the church did want (Buruma 1985, 78). The end result was that, while the church agreed that it needed to take a leadership role and deal directly with political issues, it was unclear as to what exactly its position should be. The church, and the priests, ended up in a dilemma: "Either the church, as an agent of change, loses credibility with desperate people demanding radical solutions or simply protection, or a priest is forced to do something radically opposed to the tenets of his faith" (79).

When asked what effect the church's active opposition to the

Marcos regime had on the church itself, informants' responses ranged from dramatic change to little change. Conservative and moderate informants were more likely to say that the change was great and that it improved the church, while more leftist informants complained that not much had really changed within the institution.

After 1983, although the left branch of the church was still a small minority, the institution as a whole had shifted to the Left. Eight informants stressed how the church's political involvement renewed it. They mentioned that the "church as an institution gained esteem," that its credibility increased, that it "decided that this was what it should have been doing all along," that "it was the best thing that ever happened to us," that "for some members, it became an inspiration," that political involvement "awakened us," increased the church's consciousness, made it "more relevant to the life of its faithful and more true to its nature as a Christian church." One priest said that the political situation "called us into the arena of battle. We have to fight. If we are not fighting, we are dead. We see souls [being destroyed]—we must fight." One brother said that involvement in politics "made the church people realize that they have a lot to [learn about] the situation of the country and they have a chance to do the very task they should do to fulfill their commitments for the church and the people." As one Sacred Heart sister said, "Before that, the church was not in touch with the people. It was middle class, elitist. We were conscienticized. When the church sector entered [the events of 1986], we were a very credible moral support. We were a strong moral power—in the polls, in the streets. People took strength from us."

Four informants mentioned that the effect of political activity was less a spiritual reawakening than the church's transformation as a political actor: it had the authority "to play a leading role in social issues," to push for reforms, and to have the church's position appreciated by the people. They were proud of the fact that the church did not "go for just charity but [we] directly look for the cause, go to the roots of the problems." One bishop mentioned the importance of the church supporting the organizing of BCCs as an avenue to change.

Three informants stressed that such involvement was good for the church because it was a way to create a common ground between the institutional church and the individual church. They were particularly proud of the church having taken strong stands against human rights violations and in support of the poor, the oppressed, and the underprivileged. However, they also mentioned the importance of the fact that the change was done in a conciliatory fashion. One priest said that the "church crossed the line of politics, through moral involvement." A cardinal said, "We must pray, but we must also make it relevant to people."

However, seventeen informants argued that political involvement had a negative effect on the church. Twelve informants said that the changes had fragmented the church. Three said political involvement caused confusion as to what the church's role should really be. Two openly worried about what the future ramifications would be of the church entering politics. Two informants were particularly concerned about a backlash in the form of anticommunist hysteria. Two informants admitted that there had been a widening of the split within the church but argued that this was not necessarily a bad thing. One informant said that it forced the church to rethink its beliefs and then try to mediate between and unite contradictory groups. A leftist sister pointed out that it is inevitable that some "facets of the church are more progressive than others. This is healthy. [Is it a] healthy debate in the church or a split in the church? Different people take different sides regarding what it is."

Finally, one leftist priest argued that there had been no real change within the church. While it may have adopted political tasks up to 1986, this change was not permanent and did not affect the everyday operations of the institution. "There is still the hierarchical church. [Priests] still look to bishops. The bishops are conservative. Regarding the structure of the church, nothing much has really changed."

When asked how the church's role had changed, informants mentioned the shift away from teaching and toward action. The initial role was traditional, whereby church members tried to influence people through moral teaching. They focused their attention on schools and pastoral services. They did not confront social change, nor did they try to structurally analyze their society. Any involvement in politics was minimal, with most of the church's effort going into telling people to vote wisely.

When asked what the church did, when it became active, informants offered a range of roles that the church filled, from traditional teaching tasks to identification with the poor and political involvement. The traditional tasks included church-sponsored publications, information drives, and seminars (mentioned by ten informants), lobbying laity to become involved in politics, and social action programs (mentioned by six informants). Socioeconomic tasks included solidarity with the poor (mentioned by three informants), community organizing (mentioned by three people), and pastoral work and the expansion of BCCs (mentioned by five informants). Two tasks mentioned concerned changing the church itself: conscientization and the use of structural analysis.

Political tasks of the church included participation in the Church-Military Liaison Committee; the creation of cause-oriented groups, especially task forces and human rights groups; working for clean elections (mentioned three times); speaking out against or being more critical of the regime (mentioned by four informants); engaging in processions, rallies, prayer rallies, marches, the confetti revolution, the tarmac march (to protest the Aquino assassination), and NAMFREL (mentioned by five); and mobilizing people and asking for social justice. One informant mentioned the change in the church itself in adopting a more prophetic role. One bishop mentioned the power and authority the church had in taking on political tasks "because of the credibility of the church. The church has more credibility than lay people. When the church asks people [to do something], the people will believe them."

CONCLUSION

The Philippine church's role was gradually transformed from religious mission to political activism. As more groups within the institution moved toward political activity, the church eventually felt compelled to openly oppose the Marcos regime in order to reunify itself. The legacy of authoritarianism for the church is that the church became accustomed to political activism. As we see in chapter 8, even after the regime fell, groups within the church believed that the institution should still try to directly influence policy and policymakers. Thus, the church's experience under authoritarianism, particularly in overthrowing the Marcos regime, caused the church to fragment and to remain in the political arena. Chapter 5 shows that the Philippine military underwent a parallel transformation.

5 Marcos and the Military

INTRODUCTION

■ The Philippine military's role progressed from one of professionalism, whereby the institution followed civilian supremacy, to overt political activity, first to support the Marcos regime and later to overthrow it. As with the church, the impetus for this role change was both internal and external to the institution. This change in the military's role began before martial law, with the introduction of the national security doctrine, which encouraged the military to undertake socioeconomic tasks as a counterinsurgency strategy. However, the military was also encouraged to adopt a political role by the Marcos regime, both to support the government and to suppress opposition. This change in the military's role caused the institution to fragment across several lines: junior versus senior officers, professionals versus politicos, Marcos's provincemates versus non-Ilokanos, Philippine Military Academy graduates versus enlisted men. By the early 1980s, professional soldiers realized that the only way to reunify the institution was to take a political position. Thus, conflict within the military eventually led it to overthrow the regime that it had initially protected.

FROM PROFESSIONALISM TO NATIONAL SECURITY

Traditionally, the Philippine military has been a professional institution (Hernandez 1979, 186). Prior to martial law, the military took a position of nonintervention in politics. The 1935 constitution prohibited the military from entering into partisan political activity (Hernandez 1985b, 174). The institution was set up by the Americans in 1936 and patterned after the U.S. military: it was "small, professional and committed, above all, to the notion of civilian supremacy" (Jenkins 1983a, 15). After World War II, it saw its primary role as securing the country against external threat.

When asked how the military's role in politics differed from its previous role, all of the informants stressed the professional nature of the institution. They said that it had concerned itself purely with military matters, such as security and counterinsurgency. It saw itself as being strictly professional: it followed the line of command and was disciplined. Its relations with politicians were purely subservient—the military followed civilian supremacy and supported and defended the civilian government.

The Hukbalahap (or Huk) rebellion in 1950, discussed below, caused the institution's role to expand from professional to political tasks. The expansion of the military's role brought a corresponding growth in its size, from 37,000 men and a $70.8 million budget in 1948 to 59,000 men with a budget of almost $572 million in 1970 (Hernandez 1985b, 162). When asked to pinpoint the start of military involvement in political issues, one informant said that the military had always been involved, "from the days of Quezon" (Quezon was president of the Philippine commonwealth in 1935). However, seven out of thirty-three informants mentioned the 1960s and one said military involvement began before martial law. Six informants mentioned that the expansion of the military's roles into socioeconomic projects, as part of a counterinsurgency plan, caused the military to become political.

In 1950, the military shifted its defense role from external threat to national security in response to the Huk rebellion, an uprising by an agrarian-based guerrilla group fought in central Luzon. This role expansion was introduced by the United States, which suggested the training of the military in socioeconomic issues and its adoption of civic action programs to defend against insurgency threats. The military still paid attention to traditional warfare strategies, especially through the Military Assistance Program, whereby the United States trained approximately fifteen thousand promising Philippine officers from 1950 to 1985 (Hernandez 1985b, 162). However, after 1950, military training was expanded to include "managerial skills," as the Armed Forces of the Philippines (AFP) began to introduce socioeconomic programs to counter the grassroots attraction to the Huks' agrarian reform position. The National Defense College of the Philippines was created in 1966, offering a master's in national security administration and enrolling military officers, government officials, and businessmen (183–84).

After initial failures in fighting the Huks, the AFP isolated two areas where it could act and improve its chances. First, the AFP was hampered by an image problem, due to severe problems with corruption and lack of discipline (particularly concerning the abuse of civilians). The AFP realized that it would not be able to effectively fight a popular movement if it were also alienating the mass public. To alleviate the problem, Defense Minister Magsaysay instituted a public relations cleanup of the institution. He improved public opinion of the AFP by stressing a strict discipline campaign within the military. Magsaysay himself, in a few highly publicized civilian abuse cases, disciplined the military men. He also replaced upper-level officers with junior officers who were more professional (Bello 1987, 17). The military's image was also improved by its involvement in the 1951 elections, which "were relatively clean, and they succeeded in giving the military a new image as the 'defender' of the democratic process. More important, the immediate impact of the elections was to 'open again elections as alternatives to rebellion' " (15).

Second, the military, under Defense Minister Magsaysay, realized that the war against the Huks would not be won with purely military tactics (Bello 1987, 7). It decided that it needed to add a civil action program to its military offensive against the rebels to encourage the mass public to shift its support from the Huks to the AFP (Hernandez 1985b, 161). Thus, Magsaysay began to use the AFP for socioeconomic projects.

Military civic action activities in the 1950s included infrastructure construction and repair, resettlement of landless families through the Economic Development Corps (EDCOR), digging of artesian wells, rural health programmes, building of schools, provision of better agricultural technology and extension of free legal services to the farmers, and relief operations in disaster areas. (Hernandez 1985b, 161)

This tactic was a huge success for the government. Like the discipline campaign, it did not matter how large the effort was; in the case of EDCOR, only a fraction of the rebel families, around five thousand, were relocated (Bello 1987, 15). What mattered was that the AFP was seen as working to improve the day-to-day conditions of the lives of average Filipinos.

When asked why the military became involved in political tasks when it did, two people mentioned Magsaysay's orders for the military to ensure honest elections and his personal selection of officers for promotion. Three informants mentioned politicians or political parties, since the military had to court politicians in order for individuals to be promoted and for the institution's budget to be protected. Two informants mentioned that the military became political when it was given civilian functions to perform.

Of those informants who said that the military became involved in politics before 1972, three said that the military acted to protect peace and order, to defend the government, and to resettle surrendering Huks. One said the military lobbied political parties for favors. Three mentioned that the military took on developmental roles, including some that were traditionally carried out by civilians: nation building, development, teaching, and local government (barangay captains and mayors).

Six informants stressed that while the military was given civic roles to fill, its involvement in politics was "the exception rather than the rule." Its civilian roles were limited to counterinsurgency tasks, such as civic action programs, and peacekeeping. One outside informant said that the military had "civic functions, but they do not confer a sense of power to the military." One general said that the "military has always been apolitical [but] always politically aware."

Two informants mentioned that it was only under Marcos's presidencies, from 1965 to 1971, that the military changed, because Marcos "began to shape the military as a tool for martial law. . . . He gave them perquisites of power." Marcos expanded the role of the military after he was elected to the presidency in 1965. A newspaper editor said that "Marcos expanded the role of civic action. This was part of his design to gain the support of the AFP," to control the population. In 1966, Marcos released his "Four Year Economic Program," which specified that the AFP would be one of the key governmental bodies that would be involved in socioeconomic projects. Marcos listed the new areas in which the military would be used for civilian development projects: infrastructure, "education, sanitation, agriculture, and cottage industry training" (Hernandez 1985b, 183). During Marcos's second term, the chief of staff of the AFP openly changed the military's role, formalizing its already long-standing experience in civilian work. Thus, it would now be responsible for defense against not only external threats but also internal threats and for socioeconomic development.

The view held among officers is that the military profession is no longer restricted to the task of management of violence, because violence is inseparable from the social and psychological conditions which brought it into being. The soldier must fight not only the enemies of the state but also poverty and social injustice; this task leads him to such fields as medicine, dentistry, education, construction, economic activities, and the like. (Hernandez 1985b, 172)

Thus, the military adopted a political role even before authoritarianism was installed. As we see below, this movement was greatly accelerated under the Marcos regime.

THE IMPACT OF AUTHORITARIANISM
ON THE MILITARY

After 1972, the military began to expand from being a tool of the civilian government to being a partner with the civilian ruler. It began to take on more and more tasks originally considered civilian, such as development projects, and traditionally prohibited to the military, such as adjudication.

Of the informants interviewed, sixteen dated the military's involvement in political tasks to 1972, when Marcos declared martial law. They mentioned that the military became politicized because it implemented martial law, it was the basis of support for Marcos's regime, and it closed down political institutions. A retired navy commander mentioned that Marcos corrupted the military because he "chose a few officers and gave them power." A retired colonel mentioned that after martial law, military officers were forced to become political in order to be promoted. One journalist said that the "military was always politicized. They were always appointed by political appointments. The merit system wasn't considered. The chief of staff was seen as a political protege of the president. The claim that the AFP pre-Marcos was professional is exaggerated. But they never actually played a political role before."

This role expansion was due to Marcos asking the military to move into the vaccuum he had created by closing down Congress, outlawing political parties, and calling for the resignation of all public servants. Under martial law, the military began to move from being an influencer in politics to being a key player (Hernandez 1985b, 190–91). As a result of martial law, then, the military felt important, according to three informants, because it felt it had a role to play in the restructuring of the country. It had high hopes that its participation in martial law would help the country, because it noticed that the tiger economies (such as Taiwan, South Korea, and Singapore) had authoritarian governments.

When Marcos declared martial law in 1972, he formally based his authority to rule on the 1935 constitution. However, informally he based it on the loyalty and strength of the military to depoliticize the mass public, neutralize politicians, and implement his policies. Marcos elevated the military, offered it incentives to remain loyal to himself, and expanded its roles into those normally held by civilians. Defense Minister Enrile and high-level military officers were brought into Marcos's inner circle for policy decision making. Those officers whose loyalty Marcos distrusted, or whom he wanted out of the way in order to elevate others, were removed. In 1976, eight generals were retired and twenty-one high-ranking officers were reassigned (Wurfel 1977, 24). The new echelon of military officers realized and relished their elevation over politicians and bureaucrats who prior to 1972 had controlled their budget and their behavior. The military emerged as the new political and social elites in society (Abueva 1979, 39).

Junior officers and enlisted men also saw a dramatic increase in their pay, with commissioned officers receiving a 150 percent raise in base pay (Wurfel 1977, 24). The military as an institution received benefits, as Marcos increased its budget and its size. Against the complaints of bureaucrats, Marcos increased the military's share of the budget from 13.4 percent in 1972 to 21.8 percent in 1975 (25). To retain the military's loyalty and to ensure its ability to carry out his orders, Marcos significantly increased their size. The AFP ballooned in size from 55,000 in 1972 to 164,000 in 1977 and almost 250,000 by 1985 (Hernandez 1985b, 189; Bello 1987, 31; Jenkins 1983a, 15; Aquino 1982, 196).

More importantly, Marcos expanded the military's role from securing the country not only from external threat but in particular from internal threat. This expansion meant that the military was responsible not only for depoliticizing the population but also for enforcing all of Marcos's "laws, decrees, orders, and regulations issued by the President as Commander-in-Chief of military forces" (Hernandez 1985b, 185). The military also "protected" the regime during the 1978 legislative elections and the 1980 local elections, when it was ordered to ensure victories for the KBL (Kilusang Bagong Lipunan) ticket (Vokey 1981, 28).

The military was also expanded in scope, as the police were placed under the command of the Philippine Constabulary (PC), and the ceremonial Presidential Security Command (PSC), under General Fabian Ver, took over intelligence operations (Hernandez 1985b, 186). The sudden elevation of the military was justified as corresponding with the regime's goals of law and order and economic development. As one government spokesman said, "Since we [in the Marcos administration] have adopted *discipline* as a necessary element of national progress, and since discipline has long been associated in our minds with the military way of life, it is but natural that the military now looms so vividly in our thinking" (Abueva 1979, 39).

After 1972, Marcos also gave the military roles normally filled by politicians, bureaucrats, judges, and businessmen. Marcos changed the institution's structure to ensure that he personally had control over the military. Once this was accomplished, he used the military as his political base of support and his mechanism to control political participation throughout the country. Fourteen informants mentioned specifically political tasks that the military took on. They listed filling government positions (including local government positions), campaigning during elections, transforming the Presidential Security Guard into a political body, forming cause-oriented groups, and intervening in elections to prevent violence.

Military personnel rose in status as a result of Marcos's elevation of them (Kessler 1989, 125). Once shunned by society, military officers were courted after 1972. They began to be lobbied by the mass public for privileges and favors, as local politicians had once been lobbied (Bello 1987, 34). They received the unofficial privileges "once reserved for local officials and police—the numbers and gambling rackets, for instance—were rendered unto martial law's enforcers" (Vokey 1981, 28). Military officers, across all ranks, were allowed to develop business interests on the side, including much sought-after logging rights (Jenkins 1983a, 16).

As under Magsaysay, but on a much wider basis, the military was used to develop the infrastructure. The AFP "built thousands of school buildings, provided medical and dental services to millions, reforested hundreds of hectares of land, constructed many infrastructure projects, provided relief to victims of disasters, engaged in rural electrification, land resettlement, food production and education" (Hernandez 1985b, 188). They also acted as government officials in agencies and local government. For example, military officers (retired and active) were named as ambassadors, Presidential Regional Officers for Development (PRODs), governors, and loan collectors for the land bank (Hernandez 1985b, 187–88; Jenkins 1983a, 16; Stauffer 1979, 200).

When asked what the military did, eleven informants mentioned the expansion of socioeconomic tasks: running companies, being regional development officers, and conducting civil engineering and medical programs at the local level. One mentioned nation building in general. One informant said that such roles were useful to improve public relations, showing that military personnel were citizen-soldiers who served their country beyond the military sphere.

The military's judicial role came about through the creation of military tribunals to try subversion cases during the first two years of martial law (Abueva 1979, 41). By 1974, these tribunals were slowly phased out and cases were rerouted to civilian courts.

However, crimes involving subversion, rebellion, espionage, illegal possession of firearms and explosives for use in the commission of murder, robbery in band, usurpation of military authority, title, ranks, or illegal use of military uniforms and insignia, offenses committed by military personnel in the performance of duty, distribution of subversive materials, and crimes undermining the security of the country continued to fall under the jurisdiction of military commissions which replaced the tribunals in 1978. (Hernandez 1985b, 186)

The military also filled the role of business managers in state corporations. In 1972, after the declaration of martial law, Marcos had the business empires of certain elites confiscated on the grounds that it was necessary to the country's national security that the regime own them. The Jacinto Group was taken, as well as the publishing and public utilities firms of the Lopez family and the military-related industries of the Elizalde family (Abueva 1979, 44). Once confiscated, military officers were placed on the boards of directors to run these companies (Hernandez 1985b, 187; Vokey 1981, 28).

This widening of the institution's sphere of influence, under orders from Marcos, was supported by changes in the military's training in its own education centers. The Command and General Staff College added social science and public administration courses to its curriculum, such as "Political Dimensions of National Security" and "National Security Planning, Strategy, and Policy." The military also encouraged officers to go to civilian institutions for professional degrees, such as the master's in business administration. The idea was for the military to learn the same skills that bureaucrats do, since under martial law they would be involved not only in enforcing the president's orders but also in developing his policies (Hernandez 1985b, 176). Most of the military's older officers had already gone through training in the United States and this practice was continued under martial law, with over 250 officers annually training in the United States under the International Military Education and Training program (Jenkins 1983a, 16).

When asked what was the effect of role change on the military, five respondents said that the addition of socioeconomic tasks had an empowering effect on the institution. One retired colonel said it made the military feel important, feel that it was an important part of the nation-building effort of the government. The military was sent to the United States for training and placed in government agencies. This provided the military with a new image and a new role: it was working "as an instrument of the will of the people." Military personnel felt they were useful: a retired navy commander said that they felt they were "not just soldiers carrying guns, killing people." However, this socioeconomic role also gave the military a new idea, because it saw for itself the weaknesses of government services. One general said that this "idea [was] pursued by Honasan, and silently by some elements in the military. This idea is that the military has the capability to intervene politically in the affairs of the country when things are not right or when things are not doing so well, such as the actions and activities of the political leadership of the country."

Ten informants said that martial law gave the military a new-found sense of power and a political ideology. The military was made to feel that it was not subordinate to civilian power, but rather that it had its own power based on arms. The military felt important, in terms of increased social status and new political power. A retired general said that military officers and others felt that

for once they were lording it over those [who had lorded it over them] before—politicians, Congress, or those in the military who had connections. They thought this was a chance to assert themselves. Marcos gave them the feeling that as long as they did his bidding, they would be powerful. Favors were extended to them—by Marcos, the First Lady, Ver. They felt important. They became politicized—they became aware of the role that they [played] and of the overall national situation. Marcos made [the military man] understand that the country could not stand without the military. The military was finally at the center stage.

CONFLICT AND CHANGE WITHIN THE MILITARY

Despite this dramatic expansion of the military's duties, and in particular its escalation from professional to political tasks, some people did not believe that the military would actually intervene in politics. There were three general reasons offered for why the Philippines would not follow the Thai or Indonesian model, whereby the military took power and set up a military junta. First, people pointed to the military's commitment to civilian rule, a belief entrenched under American rule. Second, the military, while it had increased its social status under martial law, was still an outsider in Philippine society. The military would not be able to gain political power without support from the elite, and it was assumed that this scenario would not occur. Third, while the military had taken on traditionally civilian roles, especially those of bureaucrats and businessmen, it had yet to prove itself as equal to or better than its civilian counterparts (Jenkins 1983a, 16).

Several factors proved these arguments wrong. First, the military over time was becoming increasingly fragmented and frustrated over its role. There were deep divisions over whether or not the military should remain political. There was deep resentment that the military was unsuccessful in carrying out its fundamental task of maintaining law and order. Second, the military increasingly believed that Marcos's leadership was harming the military, through his encouragement of divisiveness in the military and his concern that the military not threaten his own power.

As a result of this fragmentation and eroding loyalty within the military, Marcos began to take a cautious approach. Regarding the military's traditional role of maintaining law and order, the regime was selective in the freedom of action that it gave the military. On the one hand, the regime gave the military a free hand against the political opposition, especially to detain people on suspicion of subversion, which was broadly defined. Its behavior became so aggressive that it was cited early in the regime by Amnesty International for high levels of human rights abuses (Amnesty International 1976). Against the New People's Army (NPA), the military was "said to use violence indiscriminately and without regard to political consequences. They have the reputation of trying to bludgeon a community into submission if it is suspected of harboring the NPA, and they tend to rely upon the example of massive firepower to influence people rather than on its selective application" (Bello 1987, 36).

On the other hand, the military felt that Marcos was also hindering its ability to carry out its fundamental role of protecting national security, because Marcos was not allowing it to follow a total war strategy in Mindanao against the Moro National Liberation Front (MNLF) and was allowing the rebels to surrender and keep their weapons (Wurfel 1977, 27). Explaining his strategy against the MNLF, Marcos told the armed forces to "shoot only when fired upon" so as not to sabotage the ongoing peace negotiations (Marcos: The Safety Catch Is Released 1975, 12).

It was becoming clear that the AFP was not trained, equipped, or disciplined enough to defeat the rebels. Even when Marcos later allowed the AFP to take a more aggressive stand against the rebels, he admitted that his troops were not better equipped (Marcos: The Safety Catch Is Released 1975, 12). A more cynical viewpoint suggested that Marcos was willing to risk a drop in morale in order to ensure that the stronger military that he had created would not become too attached to political tasks and try to gain even more power or even take power away from him. "Some observers contend that the continuance of a moderate level of conflict in Mindanao is indirectly beneficial to Marcos, by justifying larger and larger defense expenditures and at the same time keeping the military distracted from attention to problems and opportunities in Manila" (Wurfel 1977, 27).

In 1978, Marcos tried to solve the discipline problem within the AFP by reorienting the government's slogan of *Isang Bansa, Isang Diwa* (One Nation, One Spirit) into an opportunity for the military to strengthen its discipline. This program was also devised to mend the military's image, which was one of "rampant military abuses against civilians, indiscipline that often breaks out in intraservice armed clashes (especially between the army and national police) and in soldiers running amok, in many cases recently in the southern Philippines and other areas of insurgency" (Ocampo 1978b, 37).

One outside informant said that the military became political in 1978 when, she claimed, reformist groups within the AFP began to emerge. Three informants said that the military became political in reaction to Marcos. They portrayed the military as oppressed by Marcos and Fabian Ver, complaining that Ver's group monopolized privileges. They also pointed to poor military planning causing young soldiers to be sent up to the battle front unprepared and low morale from soldiers tired of killing people. Two outside informants mentioned partisan roles that the military played. They pointed to the Ilokanization of the military, whereby Marcos promoted officers from his home province to occupy key positions both across the armed forces and within regional commands. They mentioned the need to prove one's personal loyalty to specific politicians in order to gain appointments and higher pay.

To minimize the effect of such dissent, the institution was reorganized to ensure the regime's control over the command structure and to weed out potentially disloyal commanders. Under orders from Marcos, Ver reorganized the command structure of the AFP in 1984, changing the four zone commands into thirteen regional ones (Tasker 1986a, 27; Kessler 1989, 119). These new zones were called regional unified commands: they approximated the political boundaries drawn after 1972 and they gave the commanders political influence in each region (Ocampo 1978b, 38; Sacerdoti 1984b, 16). Officers known to be loyal to

Ver were appointed to head these new commands (Tasker 1984b, 39).

Marcos also began to isolate Defense Minister Enrile, AFP Chief of Staff Romeo C. Espino, and his successor, General Fidel Ramos, from the chain of command because he did not trust them. In 1978, Marcos released, under a limited circulation, Letter of Instructions No. 776, which barred Enrile and Espino from assigning and promoting military personnel. "No change of assignment of senior officers, including provincial commanders, brigade commanders and division commanders and special unit commanders, shall be made without prior clearance from the President" (Arillo 1986, 132). In 1983, before Marcos underwent kidney surgery, he further increased Ver's powers by appointing him the only person in charge of troop movements (Sacerdoti 1984b, 16).

The AFP general staff was also reorganized, by "compartmentalization," so that each member only knew his own tasks and not what others were responsible for. Ver also forced officers to spy on each other and had their phone wiretapped (Bello 1987, 41). In this way, Ver hoped to diminish the probability of staff members allying against the regime, keep potentially disloyal members out of positions of power, and hold for himself all decision-making powers. The result of this reorganization was a further fragmentation of the military. It increased unrest within the military, as officers began to realize that they were distrusted and that they were outside of the real chain of command. It also made the institution more inefficient by creating "competing and overlapping hierarchies" (41). By 1981, Enrile was training his own army, to defend himself against Ver (Arillo 1986, 136–37).

Thus, notwithstanding the significant gains in power and prestige that the military saw after 1972, by the late 1970s dissent within the military began to rise and morale to drop. Those members who had initially resisted martial law because it was outside of the military's traditional, professional role were becoming alienated from the regime. They felt that Marcos was not allowing them to effectively end the rebellions in the country. "Some resented early restraints on military operations in the south imposed by Marcos, leadership failings that led occasionally to cavalier handling of the rebels and wholesale slaughter of green trainees, and the amnesty programme under which tens of thousands of rebels have been rewarded for surrendering, some of them several times" (Vokey 1981, 30).

They complained that the regime's policy of sudden expansion of the military without proper training and the immediate sending of these troops to Mindanao without discipline resulted in human rights abuses. "Troops, especially those in the south, were accused of looting, raping and 'salvaging,' a euphemism employed by army men to describe the murder of civilian suspects" (Jenkins 1983a, 15). Even those who had not been against martial law from the start began to have doubts by the early 1980s because of the inability of the military to end the rebellion in Mindanao.

While some officers were reaping the benefits of a politicized institution, many were not. Generals were the most advantaged under the regime. Marcos kept senior officers in their positions beyond the three-year rotation rule (Jenkins 1983a, 15). He also extended their contracts: in 1981, over half of the seventy-six generals had their contracts continued beyond their retirement age and service time (Ocampo 1981b, 12). Marcos realized the junior officers' resentment but postponed retiring the generals because the promotions would force him to choose between Ramos's and Ver's camps. For the position of chief of staff, Marcos would have to choose between Ramos and Ver themselves. Marcos was indecisive on the issue. In 1980, he promised that generals would be retired. However, he later reneged on the promise (Vokey 1981, 30). Finally, in mid-1981, Marcos relented by retiring his chief of staff and promoting Ver to that position (Ocampo 1981b, 12).

The fight over retirements and promotions expanded to become not just a question of junior versus senior but also professional versus political. It also expanded beyond the institution, with politicians and bureaucrats siding with either Ramos or Ver. On the professional side were Enrile, Ramos, Finance Minister Cesar Virata, and Industry Minister Roberto Ongpin. On the political side were Ver and Imelda Marcos. In the past, Enrile had refused to extend the generals' contracts; however, the generals were able to circumvent Enrile by going to Ver (Vokey 1981, 30). In this way, the break between the generals and the colonels, and between Enrile and Ver, was accentuated. By choosing to replace Espino with Ver, Marcos opted for someone who was personally loyal to him, and who was not influenced by the United States (Ocampo 1981b, 12).

Although the military's size and budget share were expanded, military personnel were still angry over the issue of basic pay. In 1981, "A PMA graduate who starts as a second lieutenant gets a base pay of ₱850 (US$107) per month. . . . A colonel gets about ₱2,425 while a brigadier-general get ₱3,112 basic pay. Enlisted personnel get a basic pay of ₱316–520 a month, while trainees' pay varies between ₱603 for PMA cadets and ₱316 for draftees" (Ocampo 1981b, 12).

This low pay was made worse by Marcos's distribution of privileges, such as lucrative contracts and businesses, on the basis of personal loyalty to Marcos. Non-Ilokano officers resented their inability to rise to positions of power. This suspicion of discrimination was supported by a World Bank report stating that most of the Presidential Security Command, the Philippine Constabulary and army units based near Manila, as well as eighteen of the twenty-two Philippine Constabulary generals were Ilokanos. While this strategy of promotion was increasing the rift within the military, it was considered crucial not only for Marcos but for his supporters. Not only did promotion on the basis of loyalty increase the security of Marcos's own regime, it also influenced who would become Marcos's successor, based on which politicians had the greatest number of proteges in key positions (Vokey 1981, 29).

There was also fragmentation within the military "depending on whether they are graduates of the Philippine Military Academy (PMA), activated from the reserves, trained abroad or recruited from other sources" (Vokey 1981, 30). There were instances of army and Philippine Constabulary troops shooting each other in Mindanao (Jenkins 1983a, 15). Ver was supposed to have the backing of reservists and enlisted men, who were the majority of military personnel, while Ramos was presumed to have the support of regular officers, who were graduates of the PMA (Ocampo 1981b, 12).

One theory was that Marcos encouraged fragmentation within the military, to a certain extent, in order to keep it divided and fighting within itself rather than united and fighting him. However, he underestimated the effect of low morale on the military, especially on junior officers. Opposition politicians sensed this widening dissent and began to build bridges to the junior officers, just as officers began seeking out the opposition politicians (Neher 1981, 270; Vokey 1981, 29–30).

The military became intoxicated with its increased power under martial law and, consequently, began to abuse it. One informant, a journalist, said that the military started to look at other Asian countries where the military is preeminent, like Indonesia and Thailand, to see how the military behaved. It started to have ambitions to govern. One general said that among "the lower ranks, especially the rank and file, it began to dawn on them—their power, their importance. . . . Some of the soldiers began to think that because of their power, they can impose certain decisions on other people."

A journalist said that members of the Reform the Armed Forces of the Philippines Movement (RAM) were just like all the other corrupt officers—they were acting for themselves. He claimed that they were only against Marcos because he did not give them what they thought they deserved. However, a general held the more popular view, that in "the minds of idealistic young men, RAM projected the image of leadership. They projected themselves romantically."

Six informants stated that Marcos politicized the military, by asking it to maintain his regime rather than the constitution. He also politicized it by personally interfering in the military's hierarchy. Nine informants said that the effect of the military's politicization was increasing public disaffection for and a weakening of the institution. While the military became stronger and was influential in practically all of the ministries, after 1972 "people considered generals corrupt [and] fools." The result was low morale due to the military's having become partisan, rampant with favoritism, corrupt, undisciplined, and dependent on politicians for advancement. It became unprofessional. Three informants said that the military's role change caused it to become factionalized. Five informants said that the result was the call for reform in the military. Three said that the role change caused the formation of RAM. When it held meetings, RAM said that its agenda was to search for professionalism; however, its covert agenda was to plan political intervention and the events of 1986.

MILITARY OPPOSITION TO THE MARCOS REGIME

From 1983 to 1986, conditions within the military deteriorated rapidly, due to rising levels of dissent within the institution and increasing suspicions over Marcos's health. Pro-Marcos and anti-Marcos forces became polarized. On the one hand, the Reform the Armed Forces of the Philippines Movement was created by pro-Enrile and pro-professionalism officers, in reaction to Marcos's and Ver's reorganization of the institution. On the other hand, Ver and Imelda Marcos began to jockey for post-Marcos political advantage.

Four informants said that the military did not consider a political role until 1986. One informant said that the AFP had never been involved in politics. Only one of these informants, a gen-

eral, said that the military changed in 1986 due to public demand. "The military as an organization, an institution only
supported what was perceived to be a general sentiment of the
people. The military only responded to what was perceived to be
the common will."

By 1986, the military had become top-heavy, was poorly
trained and equipped, was rampant with corruption, and was
used more and more for political goals. First, the number of officers had grown from a few thousand to fourteen thousand. Over
half of the one hundred generals, by 1985, were extendees. Second, although the military had swollen in size to 250,000, only
eighty thousand were actually "combat effective" (Bello 1987,
39–41). Third, the expansion of the military's budget, while dramatic, was not enough to cover the larger military's costs. As a
result, part of

the pay and allowance of enlisted men were "siphoned off into the
pockets of senior officers at various levels of command." Upper-level
corruption and the budgetary crunch led to incidents such as troops
refusing to engage the NPA in combat for fear that they would die for
lack of medical facilities and soldiers on patrol stealing food from civilians because they had few field rations. (Bello 1987, 40)

The Reform the Armed Forces of the Philippines Movement
was created in 1982 by five junior officers and headed by Col.
Gregorio Honasan. It grew rapidly, exceeding four thousand by
1986 (Arillo 1986, 166). RAM members claimed that they had
the support of 70 percent of the officers corps; however, independent estimates placed their membership at 1,500, out of 13,000
officers (Bello 1987, 62; Tasker 1985, 10). Most of the supporters
were PMA graduates from 1971 down and ranged in rank from
second lieutenant to lieutenant colonel. They came out in the
open in 1985 at the PMA graduation ceremonies, when three
hundred RAM members wearing We Belong T-shirts unfurled
banners on the parade ground in front of Marcos (Tasker 1985,
10–11; Arillo 1986, 168).

RAM's success was due to its refutation of the military's corruption under Marcos and its call for a reprofessionalization of the institution. RAM leaders decried "the widespread corruption in the ranks, favoritism in farming out promotions, babying of long retireable generals which stunted their own career, rampant abuses against civilians, discrimination in the allocation of supplies, and the use of military units and paramilitary units to thwart the national will at the polls during elections" (Arillo 1986, 166).

In 1985, RAM released two statements outlining the specific reforms they wanted accomplished. RAM's "Preliminary Statement of Aspirations" complained that they had

searched the leaders from among our seniors but then most, if not all, are too high to be non-partisan, too wealthy to care. Or perhaps it is their way of admitting that they no longer have the moral right to lead us to reform.

We have earlier sought to ventilate our grievances and aspirations in conventional fora, but these too have been denied us *mainly because of the prevailing military culture that has evolved in the 1980s which rewards boot-licking incompetents and which banishes independent-minded professionals and achievers* resulting in an organization with a chronic paralysis of the extremities. Subordinate commanders would rather stand idle than risk losing their comfortable positions.

This is the reason why some of us have resorted to using the alternative media. Unfortunately, some of our seniors, instead of trying to investigate this phenomenon, even went to the extent of engaging in intellectual dishonesty by dismissing everything as false and/or misrepresentations of facts. We all know who is nearest to the truth. (Aguirre 1986, 3)

RAM members also stated that they "will no longer tolerate incompetence and indiscipline. We will no longer close our eyes to the graft and corruption happening in our midst" (Aguirre 1986, 3). They wanted an end to favoritism, fragmentation within the AFP, corruption, and undisciplined personnel. They called for improved training, equipment, and supply networks, promotion based on merit, and an increase in morale (Tasker 1985). RAM members stressed that it was only through the move to professionalism that the institution would regain its ability to effectively defeat the insurgency. While some senior officers feared that RAM would accentuate growing divisions within the military, many other senior officers saw RAM as a way to finally bolster the institution's deteriorating reputation (Tasker 1985).

This solidification of opposition to the Marcos regime within the military was paralleled by an increasing effort on the part of Ver and Imelda Marcos to keep power to themselves and to keep Enrile and Ramos outside of the circle. Ver and Imelda Marcos saw Enrile as a threat to Marcos's leadership and to their own plans of succeeding Marcos; however, Enrile and Ramos realized their ambitions and were determined to stop them (Arillo 1986, 141). Marcos aided Ver and his wife in their power struggle by releasing orders that curbed Enrile's and Ramos's powers. First, he ensured that Ver and Imelda would have enough time, in the case of his death, to mobilize their forces and take control of the government, by stipulating that news of his death should be delayed by seventy-two hours. Second, Marcos transferred control of the Integrated National Police from Ramos to Ver, on August 1, 1983 (141, 142). Third, he barred Enrile and Ramos from reassigning or promoting military personnel (Sacerdoti and Tasker, 1983).

The Aquino assassination weakened the power base of Marcos and dramatically fueled the fragmentation of the military. The United States government, long a supporter of Marcos's authoritarian regime because of his anticommunist rhetoric and the fact that the United States had strategically important military bases in the country, began to distance itself from him after the assassination. The United States tried to get Marcos to make a symbolic change by formally, if not informally, replacing Ver with Ramos. However, Marcos feared that this move would increase American influence over him, and so he refused (Arillo 1986, 147). During 1984 and 1985, the United States tried to force Marcos into a compromise power-sharing scheme, again without success, whereby he would cooperate with moderate politicians toward an eventual end to authoritarian rule.

The Pentagon also stepped up its requests for reform within the Philippine military. After the Aquino assassination, the Pentagon tried to get the Philippine military to reform itself and become more professional and less political. One of the first reforms it wanted was the release of Ver and the overstaying generals (Bello 1987, 59). When that failed, the Pentagon tried to institute reforms on its own by upgrading the training program whereby Philippine officers were sent to the United States.

After a period of "neglect" during the 1970s, the Defense Department doubled the International Military Education and Training Program (IMET) allocation to nearly $1.1 million in 1982, before the crisis triggered by the Aquino assassination. By 1986, the program had again doubled to $2.2 million and involved the training of about 460 Philippine personnel annually. (Bello 1987, 60)

Marcos's refusal to compromise on the Ver or the military reform questions caused the United States government to begin to openly court the Corazon Aquino camp. They saw her as a centrist option, someone who was anticommunist but who would be willing to institute slow reform (Bello 1987, 2). During the campaign for the 1986 elections, the United States felt that it was important that Marcos appreciate the severity of the constraints placed on him. The United States fulfilled this role by "sending an observers' delegation from Congress, encouraging Western media coverage, and pressing Marcos to set up the legal framework for free elections" (64).

Finally, as political opposition to the Marcos regime rose and as his power base shrank, Marcos reassigned troops from insurgency efforts to cover his personal protection. "The Presidential Security Command alone numbered 15,000 troops nominally attached to the constabulary, or a third of the 45,000 personnel making up this branch of the armed forces. Another 10 to 12

battalions were deployed in metropolitan Manila or the area sur-
rounding it" (Bello 1987, 40).

The direct result of this deterioration was the rapid rise in the
RAM's size and power. Marcos's refusal to accede to the reforms
the United States government wanted encouraged the RAM to
continue organizing and pushing for reform from within the institution. After the Aquino assassination, RAM accelerated its efforts, linking its message of reform with a new promise that it
would neither institute nor support a coup (Arillo 1986, 167).

The Aquino assassination caused moderates within the AFP to
dissent openly. A group of thirty-one high-ranking retired AFP
officers released a statement after the assassination condemning
the suspicion it had placed on the military. It argued that the
regime must not try to protect military officers from prosecution
because such a cover-up would permanently damage the military
in the eyes of the people and prevent it from carrying out its
duties.

Since [Aquino's] assassination was executed while he was in the custody
of, and being escorted by, elements of AVSECOM [Aviation Security
Command], a unit of the Armed Forces of the Philippines, the reputation and image of the AFP has been seriously affected and blemished.
This stigma has naturally tainted the reputation of not only officers and
men in the active service, but also those who have given their lifetime
service to the nation and are now in retirement. (Tasker 1984a, 38)

A group of junior officers calling themselves the "Armed Defenders of Democracy" also released a statement after the assassination. They criticized Ver, saying that under his leadership the
number of incidents of "abuses, including involvement by certain
military figures in controlling gambling dens, smuggling and kidnapping, and protecting prostitutes" in the military had risen
dramatically (Tasker 1984a, 38).

Colonel Alexander Bacalla, the assistant deputy chief of staff
for civil-military operations, identified himself as one of the
"70% of the officer corps of the Armed Forces of the Philippines.

These are the officers who are not identified or associated with Ver, Ramos, or Enrile. They are not, therefore, beneficiaries of the prevailing system of patronage and favoritism in the Armed Forces of the Philippines" (Bacalla 1985, 3). He resigned publicly, saying that

I can no longer wear with pride the uniform I once so proudly wore. Under the Marcos dictatorship, that uniform—in the eyes of our people—drips with blood, the blood of countless victims of military atrocities—and the blood of Ninoy Aquino! Our people under the Marcos dictatorship associate that uniform with abuse of power and authority, with graft and corruption, with distorted loyalty, with loss of honor and dignity. (Bacalla 1985, 2)

The Agrava report, set up to investigate the Aquino assassination, implicated twenty-five military personnel and one civilian. One of the officers named was Ver. After Marcos personally lobbied Judge Corazon Agrava, she released a minority report that minimized military culpability. The minority report only named Aquino's six escorts and the Aviation Security Command (AVSECOM) chief, Brig. Gen. Luther Custodio (Sacerdoti 1984a, 14).

In reaction to the Agrava report, Marcos tried to build public support for Ver and to undermine the legitimacy of the report. He stated that "there is no indication that [his] administration can be overthrown by either the bullet or the ballot" (Sacerdoti 1984a, 14). Immediately after the speech, sixty-eight of the eighty-three generals in the armed forces issued a statement declaring their "unwavering loyalty and support" for Ver (14). The Aquino assassination case was eventually sent to the Sandigbayan, a court set up to judge governmental misdoings, which was controlled by Marcos. The Sandigbayan exonerated all twenty-six defendants on all fifty-two charges (Sacerdoti 1985a).

After the Aquino assassination, Marcos's ill health, the economic crisis in the country, and the open jockeying for power in a post-Marcos scenario increased the military's political power and its motivation to intervene in politics. It became evident that Ver's control over Malacangang Palace had increased. Since Marcos's kidney operation, he only allowed close advisors to visit. These included three Ilokanos: Ver, Imelda Marcos, Juan Tuvera (Marcos's executive assistant); and two cronies: Roberto Benedicto and Eduardo Cojuangco (Sacerdoti and Tasker 1983).

The military took harsh steps against the opposition after the country's reaction to the assassination. Not only did it move against the grassroots opposition movements, it also attacked those in the upper class. It tear-gassed a demonstration and noise barrage; it arrested, for 9 hours, Rogelio Pantaleon, vice-president of Ayala Corp. and publisher of an opposition magazine; padlocked *Philippine Times,* an opposition newspaper and detained Rommel Corro, its editor (Sacerdoti and Tasker 1983, 16).

Speculation rose as to whether or not the military would set up a caretaker government. Government officials informally admitted that Marcos had outlined a "secretariat" government to take over in case he had to go abroad for medical treatment after his kidney operation. Such a government included the AFP (Sacerdoti 1984b). Speculation then centered on whether the secretariat, or any caretaker government, would be run by Ver or Enrile and Ramos.

Ver's camp was considered extremely powerful. He had the backing of Marcos, of Ilokano officers, and of Marcos's supporters outside the military. He also had significant institutional bases of power: the PSC, the National Intelligence and Security Agency (NISA), the commander of the army, and the heads of the thirteen regional unified commands (Sacerdoti 1984b; Tasker 1985). While Enrile and Ramos's powers within the institution were constrained by Marcos and Ver, they still had significant power bases as well. Enrile, through his action against extendee generals, had gained the loyalty of disgruntled junior officers. Ramos's largest asset was his reputation of honesty and integrity, and his being an alumnus of the United States Military Academy. He was also supported by businessmen because of his strong civilian-supremacy position. Within the institution, he was supported by the military personnel who preferred that the military become reprofessionalized. These soldiers were usually PMA graduates who were concerned with the AFP's failure to end the insurgency and its increasing lack of discipline (Sacerdoti 1984b, 16).

Besides these two camps, there were two informal groupings of military officers that were supportive of neither camp but were waiting to see what would happen. The first informal group, which was relatively small, consisted of officers who came from the same background as the Ramos supporters but who believed that the military should in no way play a political role. They preferred that the political institutions be strengthened and that civilians prepare and administer any post-Marcos government. This group supported opposition politicians. The second informal group believed that the Philippines had to have an authoritarian government in order to run effectively. They said that while they would follow civilian rule and would support the constitution during a succession, they believed that Filipinos wanted strong leadership. However, it would be more likely that these officers would intervene in politics themselves to set up a military government if a succession government failed, even if this meant that they were acting against the wishes of the United States (Sacerdoti 1984b, 16–17).

People began to suspect that RAM had ulterior motives; that besides reforming the military, RAM was concerned about blocking a Ver-Imelda Marcos succession if Marcos died or was incapable of governing. RAM members admitted that they would block such a succession, with force if necessary. People began to fear that such political intervention to bar Ver and Imelda Marcos would cause RAM members themselves to become political actors, either through setting up their own government or at least setting themselves up as permanent political brokers (Tasker 1985, 10, 11).

Surprisingly, three informants said that the military's politicization had no influence on the military. One retired general claimed that the events of 1986 were "due only to the feelings of junior officers" but not to the feelings of the institution as a whole. One general said that there was no change at all.

When asked how the military's role differed from before it was political, one general said that the military became prominent because of martial law.

It became so prominent in society that it led to its alienation from a very large segment of society. Because there was no check and balance, no external control mechanisms, it was a system of single, national authority. Within the military itself, many of us began to see that we were moving farther and farther away from the people. And we were beginning to realize that we were being used by Marcos in a subtle way. Because Marcos' rules were worded in such a way that they agreed with the role of the military. And since the military runs on discipline, all the orders [from Marcos] were obeyed.

CONCLUSION

The transformation the military experienced moved it from a professional to a national security role. Groups within the military formed to push for political activism as Marcos's regime was increasingly seen as harming both the institution's interests and the country as a whole. Eventually, the military as an institution openly defected and called for Marcos to resign, as a way to reunify. However, political activism did not end with the collapse of the Marcos regime. As is shown in chapter 8, groups within the military tried to remain in the political arena under the Aquino government. Thus, as with the church, the authoritarian experience led to a variety of changes within the military that caused it to continue to intervene in the political arena even after the reestablishment of a democratic government. The next chapter details the actions that both the military and the church undertook to oust the Marcos regime.

6 The Collapse of the Marcos Regime

■ The dramatic events that forced President Marcos and his family to flee the country were spread over a four-day period, from February 22–25, 1986 (Aguirre 1986; Arillo 1986; Fenton 1986; Shaplen 1986a, 1986b; Johnson 1987; Wurfel 1988). The immediate catalyst for the events was the announcement by Marcos that he would hold "snap elections" in 1986. According to the constitution, presidential elections were not scheduled until 1987. However, to bolster his regime with some internal but mostly external supporters, particularly the United States, Marcos declared on the ABC program "This Week" that they would be held one year early (Mydans 1985).

Marcos saw the 1986 elections as an easy way to bolster his regime for three reasons. First, he was counting on the opposition to continue its inability to unify. With the opposition fragmented, their vote splitting would give Marcos an easy victory. Second, he assumed that the timing of the elections would catch the opposition off guard, offering them little time to organize a grassroots campaign. Finally, Marcos planned to continue his electoral system of voter fraud, intimidation, and ballot stuffing to ensure his victory (Villegas 1987, 195; Overholt 1986).

However, none of Marcos's assumptions held. First, the opposition surprised everyone by unifying behind one ticket. Initially, it seemed that Marcos's assessment of the opposition was correct.

115

Both Corazon Aquino (the widow of Senator Benigno Aquino) and Salvador Laurel registered their candidacy. They were running under different opposition parties: Aquino for *Lakas ng Bayan* (LABAN: People Power) and Laurel for the United Nationalist Democratic Organization (UNIDO). At the last minute, after heavy lobbying from Cardinal Sin, Aquino and Laurel agreed to share the same ticket (Villegas 1987, 195; Youngblood 1987a, 351).

Second, the unified ticket increased the opposition's grassroots campaigning ability. Laurel's UNIDO party already had the most extensive popular opposition organization in the country. Because of this fact, Laurel was able to convince Aquino to run as a UNIDO candidate. Aquino, because of her charisma and symbolism, was able to create a high level of voter enthusiasm, which none of the other potential opposition candidates would have been able to accomplish.

Third, Marcos's electoral modus operandi was constrained by the National Movement for Free Elections (NAMFREL), the citizen watchdog group. NAMFREL set up its own ballot-tallying system, named "Operation Quick Count," to verify returns announced by the Commission on Elections (COMELEC). It was able to undertake such an operation, in part, because NAMFREL and NAMFREL affiliates were heavily funded by businessmen, church groups, and the Agency for International Development (AID) (Villegas 1987, 195; Wurfel 1988, 298).

The elections were characterized by the regime's "monopolization of the media, intimidation of the opposition, payoffs on an extraordinary scale, efforts to deprive the opposition of funds and transport, inadequate provision of time for the opposition to organize, stolen ballot boxes, [and] mistabulation of the results" (Overholt 1986, 1161).

Voter lists disappeared: it was estimated that from 3.3 million to 5 million people were barred from entering polling places or were otherwise unable to vote (Aquino 1986, 157; Villegas 1987, 195). Election violence figures ranged from ninety-one to almost two hundred dead (Villegas 1987, 195; Aquino 1986, 156). Thirty COMELEC vote tabulators walked off the job and took refuge in a convent, claiming that Marcos was forcing them to skew the votes (Aquino 1986, 155; Villegas 1987, 195).

The results of the election were announced in Marcos's favor. When the COMELEC tabulators walked off the job, Marcos halted the COMELEC vote and turned the election over to the National Assembly for the final canvas, as delineated under the 1973 constitution. The assembly, which was controlled by Marcos's KBL party, declared Marcos the winner with 54 percent of the vote. This figure was identical to the one that NAMFREL announced as Aquino's level of support. (Aquino 1986, 155).

The response to the election result was swift. Early in the vote tabulation process, U.S. Senator Richard Lugar, who had flown to Manila as part of a U.S. delegation to watch the elections, stated that Marcos was trying to influence the elections through voter fraud and intimidation. President Reagan, after initial support for Marcos, finally agreed that the elections had not been fair and sent special envoy Philip Habib to Manila to negotiate between the Marcos and Aquino forces (Aquino 1986, 155).

Aquino refused to compromise, stating that she had won the election and that she should therefore accede to the presidency. She held a *Tagumpay ng Bayan* (People's Victory) rally, where almost one million people showed up to denounce the election results and reaffirm that Aquino was the rightful winner (Villegas 1987, 195; Aquino 1986, 155). Aquino called for a national boycott to protest the elections, to last until Marcos stepped down (Wurfel 1988, 301).

The church and the military immediately sided with Aquino, calling the election void. Close to one million people flowed into the streets to protest the election. As a result, Marcos found himself going against a widening circle of opposition, both in terms of numbers and sectors. Not only were the poor, the peasants, and the students pressing for him to step down, but so too were the church, the military, and businessmen. Finally, after a pro forma swearing-in ceremony for the presidency, Marcos, his family, and their entourage boarded a plane to Honolulu.

THE CHURCH AND REGIME CHANGE

The collapse of the Marcos regime entailed the participation of many sectors of society. That is in part why the effort was successful and Marcos fled the country. However, while many different sectors participated, the church and the military played pivotal roles in the events of 1986. Furthermore, their activity was the culmination of their changing roles under authoritarianism, from 1972 to 1986. By 1986, both the church and the military had adopted overtly political roles as a way to protect and unify their institutions.

Of the two institutions, the church was the first to openly participate in the events leading up to Marcos's overthrow. In January, the Institute on Church and Social Issues (ICSI) drafted postelection scenarios and circulated them for discussion. The scenarios included: the declaration of martial law, Marcos declared the winner of an election characterized by massive cheating, Marcos winning a clean election, the opposition winning but Marcos refusing to cede power, and the opposition winning and Marcos stepping down (ICSI 1986, 312–23). For each scenario, winning strategies were devised for five groups: the Marcos/Ver camp, the Aquino/Laurel camp, cause-oriented opposition groups, the radical Left, and the church. Scenario II, which ended up being the result of the election, raised problems for the church: "The basic moral question of whether a government 'elected' by means of massive cheating has a moral claim on the obedience of the people will . . . have to be faced by the Hierarchy" (318).

Before the 1986 election, on February 2, the Catholic Bishop's Conference of the Philippines released a pastoral letter to be read from the pulpits. It warned of a "conspiracy of evil" that was threatening to influence the elections through voter fraud (CBCP

1986a, 328). It stressed that such fraud was already underway, including registration "anomalies and flying voters, vote-buying and -selling, bribery, pressures, serious lies, black propaganda, the fraudulent casting, canvassing, and reporting of votes, snatching and unwarranted switching of ballot boxes, physical violence and killings" (Claver 1986b, 357).

Furthermore, the letter stated that "if a candidate wins by cheating, he can only be forgiven by God if he renounces the office he has obtained by fraud" (Sacerdoti 1986a, 12). Sin tried to ensure a high turnout for the snap election, since this election was perceived as a real chance for change. He told people that voting was part of the Christian faith. He tried to diminish the potential impact of fraud by stating that people should accept money for their votes, if it is offered, but that they were under no obligation to vote in any way except their conscience since the bargain would be immoral (Youngblood 1987b, 1244).

The pastoral letter had several effects. First, the bishops urged people to vote, rather than to boycott. Leftist members of the church had asked that the bishops allow people to boycott the 1986 election if this act would follow their conscience. However, the bishops wanted people not only to mark their protest against Marcos but also to vote for someone, thereby also protesting against the Communists who were encouraging a boycott (Claver 1986b, 357). They suggested that people vote for "persons who embody the Gospel values of justice, humility, truth, freedom, courage, love, peace, respect for human rights and life. Vote for persons who morally, intellectually and physically show themselves capable of inspiring the whole nation towards a hopeful future" (CBCP 1986a, 329).

The bishops were clearly not only exhorting people to vote, but to vote for Aquino (Youngblood 1987b, 1244). The COME-LEC warned the church not to try to influence voters in the presidential election. It complained that the church made it clear, without naming names, which candidate it supported (Sacerdoti 1986b, 13). Second, the church encouraged people not only to vote but also to protect their votes by securing their ballots. In particular, the bishops supported NAMFREL and its quick-count program. Third, the bishops espoused a nonviolent campaign, again not only aligning themselves with the Aquino candidacy but also distancing themselves from the Communists (Claver 1986b, 357).

After the release of the statement, Cardinal Sin personally campaigned for voter turnout. He urged the opposition to merge so as to increase the probability of overthrowing Marcos. The church used its radio station and its power of the pulpit through pastoral letters to counteract the regime's monopoly of the media during the campaign (Lande 1986, 142–43). Sin's position was not unique: he was supported by other cardinals and church members and by church organizations, such as the CBCP. The Catholic church lobbied heavily for NAMFREL to be certified for the 1986 elections and Catholics, both lay people and religious, made up a significant portion of volunteers for NAMFREL.

Approximately 20% of all national and provincial coordinators of NAMFREL were either bishops or priests, and in many provinces the provincial and municipal headquarters of NAMFREL were housed in facilities of the Catholic church, as was the national tabulation center in Manila. NAMFREL also stationed more than 600 priests and nuns—the so-called NAMFREL marines, decked out in cassocks and habits—in Manila's most notorious precincts "to intimidate the intimidators," while it mobilized over 500,000 citizens nationwide to monitor and guard the ballots. (Youngblood 1987b, 1245)

The church also supported RAM, especially its *Kamalayan* '86 (Consciousness) campaign, in part because RAM had promised that it would support the Aquino-Laurel ticket (Youngblood 1987b, 1246).

After the election, the church sided with the opposition by decrying the rampant electoral fraud. The church protected thirty technicians who walked out of the COMELEC tabulating headquarters, complaining that they were being asked to skew the election returns to favor Marcos. They brought from COME-LEC headquarters computer disks with the data to prove their accusations (Youngblood 1987b, 1247; Johnson 1987, 177).

On February 11, the ICSI again prepared a document for circulation. This time, it offered a brief analysis and suggestions of possible strategies the church could take, given the election results. It was drafted specifically for reading at the CBCP's meeting on February 13–14. This document pointed out that the Philippines was in the second scenario, with Marcos claiming he had won the election even in the face of charges of massive electoral fraud (Carroll 1986a, 332). It suggested that the church on the one hand discourage violence while on the other hand refuse to recognize Marcos as the legitimate winner of the election (333). On February 12, priests and nuns held a prayer rally and protest march against the electoral fraud. Bishops attended Aquino's *Tagumpay ng Bayan* rally to protest the election and call for civil disobedience (Youngblood 1987b, 1248).

The CBCP released a statement on February 14 that declared the 1986 presidential elections to be the worst in Philippine history in terms of electoral fraud (Claver 1986b, 358). The CBCP decided they had to take a strong position after they received overwhelming evidence regarding fraud and intimidation during the elections. They singled out the practices of erasing people from voting lists, vote buying, ballot tampering, intimidation, harassment, terrorism, and murder (CBCP 1986b, 336–37). The bishops concluded by declaring the Marcos regime null and void (Wurfel 1988, 300; Claver 1986b, 358). Specifically, they stated that "a government that assumes or retains power through fraudulent means has no moral basis. For such an access to power is tantamount to a forcible seizure and cannot command the allegiance of the citizenry" (CBCP 1986b, 337).

The bishops concluded that it was up to the regime to correct such fraud, and said that if the regime did not do so, it was the "moral obligation" of people to make the regime correct it. The church called for "active resistance of evil by peaceful means," that is, civil disobedience (Buruma 1986, 11). However, such action could only be done nonviolently (Claver 1986b, 358). "Now is the time to speak up. Now is the time to repair the wrong. The wrong was systematically organized. So must its correction be. But as in the election itself, that depends fully on the people; on what they are willing and ready to do. We, the bishops, stand in solidarity with them in the common discernment for the good of the nation" (CBCP 1986b, 338).

Bishop Claver made the message even more explicit by saying that "the church will not recognise President Marcos even if he is proclaimed winner." The reaction to the church's statement was overwhelmingly positive. The pope sent a telegram saying "I am with you." In the Philippines, when "the bishops' statement was read, congregations in many churches burst into applause" (Buruma 1986, 11).

This statement was the first time that the Philippine church had publicly stated that the regime had no choice but to step down. The CBCP postelection statement is even more remarkable given the initial attempt of Rome to halt such action. While the bishops were meeting to decide on the statement, two messages from the pope, sent through a cardinal, were read. The first asked the CBCP to exercise prudence in their meeting. This message was taken by the CBCP to mean that they should not release anything that could exacerbate the political situation. A second message was more pointed: it suggested that the bishops not release their statement until after the National Assembly had canvassed the votes and declared a winner. Rome's lobbying was quickly quashed by reference to "Octogesima Adveniens," (an apostolic letter written by Pope Paul VI in 1971) which clearly laid out the principle that "the local church has full competence to pronounce judgment on local issues" (Claver 1986b, 359). After that, the bishops continued with the drafting of their post-election statement.

Many people, including conservative members of the church

itself, criticized the CBCP for the postelection statement, claiming that the church was intervening in political matters. However, the bishops feared that their silence could also be interpreted as a political act, for by not saying anything, they would have been approving Marcos's reelection claims. "And the consequences of such a stance would have been bloodshed, violence and a continuing crisis that would have sunk the nation deeper into self-destruction" (Claver 1986c, 377). The moderates within the church were able to convince conservatives that such a statement was necessary not only to protect the country but also to protect the institutional church. It was seen as crucial to protect Aquino's claim to the presidency because she symbolized a choice between Marcos and the Communists that both the moderates and conservatives could embrace. They saw the Aquino campaign as "perhaps the last chance to undercut the drift to the Left in society, and in the church itself." The institutional church wanted to make sure that what happened in Nicaragua, where liberation theology fragmented the institutional church, did not occur in the Philippines (Buruma 1986, 12, 13). One priest said that "Cory can mobilize people without the National Democratic Front. A victory for her would delay momentum of the revolutionary movement, for there will be new hope injected in the people" (12).

However, the Left felt that the moderates within the church were deluding themselves by thinking that an Aquino presidency would allow the church to push back the leftist inroads in the institution. They argued that "local politics force the church and politicians to accommodate militants" (Buruma 1986, 13).

When Enrile and Ramos defected from the regime, the church threw its support behind them. Cardinal Sin spoke on Radio Veritas, calling for people power. He told people that the situation was dire and asked them to rush to the military camps to protect the rebels from loyalist forces. The church's radio station was used to give continuous coverage of the events during February 22–25, 1986. Ramos and Enrile used a hookup with the radio not only to publicize and strengthen their own situation but also to chip away at Marcos's position by continuously stating that he stole the election and should step down. When Radio Veritas's transmitter was destroyed by Marcos loyalist troops, the radio workers moved around Manila, transmitting on pirated stations, with nuns protecting the station in case the loyalists discovered the transmitter's location and tried to arrest June Keithley, the announcer.

After Marcos fled the Philippines, the church was faced with the question of whether to remain in the political arena or to withdraw. On March 16–17, 1986, several bishops met for a retreat to reflect on the future role of the church. They were trying to balance Aquino's request for church participation with the risk of seeming like power brokers (Claver 1986a, 363). One issue on which they were to be consulted was a list of names for the positions of officers-in-charge (OICs) who would replace local government officials who served during the Marcos years. They drafted several suggestions: to suggest several names for positions, rather than one name; to suggest qualities rather than individuals; to suggest against candidates rather than for any one particular candidate; and to offer all advice under strict confidentiality (364). In other words, the church wanted to offer advice without appearing to support any particular candidate and without appearing to have a powerful role in the establishment of the new government.

They also drafted a list of issues on which the church should participate strongly, to press for reform: land reform, protection of tribal lands, urban housing, a new constitution, reforestation, redress for human rights crimes and other crimes committed under the Marcos regime, reconciliation and amnesty, and the nurturing of people power to ensure participation, especially for the poor (Claver, 1986a, 364–65).

They also reflected on how to merge the church's pastoral tasks with the new political situation. They feared the perceptions of the people. "Church people are suddenly finding themselves cast in the role of power brokers and they are not happy with this turn of events: The Church is *malakas* [influential] with the government; the Church is in high favor with the government; the Church is a sure channel for acquiring posts in the government" (Claver 1986a, 366).

The bishops drafted a list of principles to guide the church on how to behave in the future. First, they stressed that the church's power must be used for the benefit of all in society, especially for socioeconomic reforms. Second, it must be exercised through moral suasion, not coercion. Third, it must always be used for moral purposes, since the "tempting of Christ in the desert was to this end, that He prostitute His power for sheerly political purposes" (Claver 1986a, 367). Fourth, that while the church's work has a clearly political dimension, this aspect must be fit and be subservient to its evangelical and pastoral roles. Fifth, while pulling into the background, to allow the people themselves to participate, the church must continue its prophetic role, to achieve both national reconciliation and critical collaboration (367). They concluded by saying that the church must work to change structures and values, to institutionalize mass participation, and to end political privilege for the few. They suggested that one of the best ways to achieve these goals was through expanding the number of BCCs (368–69).

Cardinal Sin visited Pope John Paul II after the February Revolution. The pope told Sin that he was worried that the Philippine church had become too politicized (Claver 1986b, 356). The pope repeated his worries in a letter sent to the CBCP for its July 1986 meeting. While the pope acknowledged the events of February and congratulated the country for the lack of violence involved in the events, he still voiced "apprehension" regarding the Philippine situation (Joanne Paulus II 1986, 392). He agreed that socioeconomic conditions in the country were dire and required the church to remain in solidarity with the poor.

This service of love and fidelity to man must however be in conformity with the nature of the mission of the Church, which is not of the temporal but of the spiritual order, not of the social, political or economic order but of the religious one. . . . This means, then, that the Church is called not to take positions of a political character, or to take part in partisan conflicts, but to give society the expert contribution which is proper to her, as the spiritual light and strength that can contribute to building and consolidating the human community. (Joannes Paulus II 1986, 392)

The pope stressed that the church must remain faithful to its evangelical mission of spreading the word of God. Thus, the church should restrict itself to raising the consciousness of the laity and unifying the country peacefully, through its teachings. The church should let the laity itself become involved in temporal, political matters (Joannes Paulus II 1986, 393). "The church's part in the revolution was, in the eyes of all, a critical element for its success. As a result, it has attained a place of honor that even its once harshest critics grudgingly concede. It is in this postrevolutionary context of high visibility and praise that a long, hard look is being taken at the church's power—its nature, exercise and scope." (Claver 1986c, 378).

However, the pope's position was not fully supported within the church. Bishop Claver suggested that the February Revolution showed the church how to act in a revolutionary way for revolutionary change without relying on Marxist ideas. He suggested that rather than withdrawing, the church should continue to identify with the people and to act with them to achieve economic change. To try to bridge the continuing gap, the CBCP released a pastoral letter in August, urging reconciliation and unity. However, the church also stressed the need for both the church and the faithful to remember to include spirituality in their actions for reform. This letter inaugurated the "one hundred days of prayer and penance" program to encourage people to focus on the country's continuing struggles (CBCP 1986c, 396–97).

However, the fragmentation of the church remained. After the February Revolution, several church groups retreated to the background (Youngblood 1987b, 1249). However, individual members of the church continued to play a strong role in the new government. Two of Aquino's closest advisors after the events of 1986 were Cardinal Sin and Father Joaquin Bernas, president of Ateneo de Manila University (Lande and Hooley 1986, 1093). Other high-visibility church officials were appointed to positions on the Constitutional Commission (ConCom), along with Bernas, or in Aquino's administration: Bernardo Villegas, an economist and Opus Dei member, and Lourdes Quisumbing, former head of Maryknoll University (Youngblood 1987a, 366). As one Jesuit said, during

The first month after the elections [of 1986], the church played a prominent role in politics. It gave recommendations to the Aquino administration for who to appoint or hire as politicians and bureaucrats. After the first month, its political activities declined. It still gave moral support to Cory. It pushed for reforms, especially land reform. But the Church didn't completely retreat from politics to pre-1983 days.

The church backed the establishment of the Constitutional Commission, the controversial body that wrote the new constitution. Many of the members of the Constitutional Commission were from the clergy (Youngblood 1987b, 1249–50). The bishops met in a special session to discuss the draft constitution and their public response to it. While voting to support the draft, they realized that "the very ratification had become a partisan issue."

The bishops chose not so much to ignore the political issue as to put it within the framework of the greater good: Voting "yes" to the Constitution would be to approve a fundamental law that on the whole—and remarkably well—conformed in their judgment to basic church social teachings; it would also go a long way toward stabilizing the national condition, a problem of no little moment, and reinstituting lost democratic processes. Again, as in their historic action in February 1986, the bishops could be said to be acting politically, not as politicians, however, but as pastors and hence within their competence as upholders of morality. (Claver 1987, 234–35)

The church saw itself as an informal champion for honesty and performance in government, via its use of the pulpit. This fact was acknowledged by aspiring officeholders, who courted the church to support their candidacy. However, while the church believed that it should press for good government, it did not want to be seen as advocating the candidacy of specific politicians or supporting specific political parties. Thus, after a meeting of several bishops, it was decided that the church should support "qualities rather than persons" (Youngblood 1987a, 367). The church also supported Aquino's national reconciliation theme, especially directed toward the insurgents. Thus, they supported the cease-fire with the CPP/NPA to negotiate a peace plan. Church members acted as intermediaries between the government and Communist groups (Youngblood 1987b, 1252). Although with less unity, the church also supported government negotiations with the MNLF (1253). Thus, members of the church, regardless of their ideological position, acknowledged that it was "one of the main social institutions propping up Mrs. Aquino's shaky Government" (Claver 1987, 234). Indeed, Bishop Claver argued that such church behavior was not any different from before 1986, when the church was in "critical collaboration" with the Marcos regime.

However, after the events of February 1986, there was a group within the church that felt that what happened on Epifanio de los Santos Avenue, or EDSA, when people streamed into the streets to defend both the rebels and Aquino's claim to the presidency, was not enough and that a second revolution was needed. This group believed that while political change had occurred—Marcos had been ousted and Aquino was now president—a social revolution had not occurred (Carroll 1986b, 10). Among the moderates of this group there was the sense that Aquino must push through certain policies to redistribute wealth and power to the lower classes so as to cut off a potential leftist revolution overthrowing the moderate one. They used the models of the "great revolutions" of Russia and China to support their argument (10–12).

The solution offered was to create a network of interest groups among the lower classes to lobby Aquino for change. To ensure that such lobbying would be heard, the concept of solidarity, as expressed by Pope John Paul II, was stressed. In this scenario, the upper and middle classes, which are more educated and more powerful, must champion the lower-class organizations' demands with national government leaders and mold public opinion, through the media, to increase societal support for social change (Carroll 1986b, 13; 1986c, 4–5). Thus, this position urged that the sense of solidarity that began at EDSA should be continued and expanded in order to gain real change. It also categorically disagreed with the Left's position of changing values and culture in order to get people to work for social change (Carroll 1986c, 6–7).

When asked what effect becoming involved in political tasks had on the church, many informants mentioned the church's participation in the events of 1986 as a positive, uplifting experience for themselves and for the institution. Eight informants said that the church's role increased the prestige of the church by bringing it closer to the people and focusing on its evangelical mission. They also mentioned that it "heightened the awareness of the church people" and "purified" the church. One religious superior rejoiced, saying that the church's work "is no longer 'faith in the head.' Now it is more with the people."

Six informants said that the experience taught the church that it should not be afraid to stand up and act. One Jesuit said that prior to the events of 1986, "the church was always afraid of Marcos's political clout. There was a threat against the church that the government would work for the legalization of abortion. So, this threat is no longer there. The church is no longer afraid that something will be taken away."

The church realized that it "has a moral role within the realms of politics," especially to work for justice, and it acted to fill that role. One priest said that there "are healthy signs in the change [in the church's work]. There are active priests and church groups, active in liberation. Because liberation is from sin, and sin is anything which is keeping us from a full life. What is a full life? I tell people that God wants them to have their own house, a car, and money in the bank."

Informants pointed to specific positions the church took, supporting Aquino's Comprehensive Agrarian Reform Program (CARP), its own preferential option for the poor, and its work through BCCs. One bishops said that "BCCs have been used by the Left—and also by the Right—why not? But in itself I think it is the ideal means for people to have the practical skills and moral support."

Three informants were optimistic that the change in the church was permanent and that the church would now try to figure out how to continue its work in the new political climate. One Jesuit priest said that the "church has learned its potential as a rallying point for the people. It wants to be able to rally people again, in the future. But it is not sure how to do this." One leftist sister pointed out that the church was now in a period of reflection, to decide how it should fill its new role.

The effect within the church is continuing the challenge, for the church to really test itself. It realizes the prophetic role it has to play this time. It is rethinking its own mission. It brings tension into the church because the conservative side will keep looking at the prophetic side with suspicion—some church people are labeled as Communists, others as not Communists. But the tension is healthy for the church and the Christian community.

A leftist priest said that the church was in a period of consolidation. "The church is a wounded healer. The church which dared to be with the people has been wounded. When the next EDSA comes, I hope it is the real people's church there. The church I belong to is preparing for the next EDSA."

However, many other informants did not see the church's role in 1986 as positive. For these informants, the church did not go far enough in 1986, and after the regime change they felt that it was returning to an apolitical role. One reason offered to explain this retreat was that since democracy had been restored, church leaders felt that the church should go back to focusing on the sacramental aspects of their work—"what they know best"—because the church could work "more as partners than as antagonists." One sister pointed out that after 1986, it was

much more difficult to work in the Justice and Peace Commission this time. It is very difficult right now because of the "Cory mystique." She is legitimately elected. With Marcos, everyone thought he was illegitimate. After 1986, those who [worked to install the Aquino government] had high hopes. So there is more splintering now. Even with religious congregations, there is the idea that if you criticize the current regime, you are destabilizing it.

The second reason was that it was seen as the right time to return to their primary tasks in order to regain church members whom the church had alienated "in carrying out its political and socioeconomic roles."

Ten informants felt that the effect of the events of 1986 was a further fragmentation of the institution. After Aquino was installed in the presidency, groups within the church began to realign. Members on the Right opposed Aquino because they feared she would introduce social reforms, such as land reform, which would harm conservative interests. However, the Right was small in number after 1986, while the center's power increased dramatically because of the nonviolent transformation from an authoritarian to a democratic government. The center and left of center began to push the Left out. The Left, like the Right, became isolated. As one sister said, "before 1986, there was a strong sympathy of the Left and far Left. Now, a bigger percentage of sisters are considering peace coalitions and getting disillusioned with the intransigence of the Left for not giving

Aquino a chance. We are still aware, though, that Aquino is not there to solve everything."

Three informants said that the effect of 1986 was that the church felt that it could go after the leftist members of the church and purge them. The increased power of the center in the church gave that group the sense that they could be anti-Left. Leftists argued that there was a higher level of repression against the church after 1986, with convents raided and church leaders jailed. One priest pointed out that

[Moreso] now than under Marcos, the number of church organizations and church people involved in social action are suspected of being sympathetic with if not collaborating with Communists is rising. This increased anticommunism is affecting people involved in the social ministry. This anticommunism is also encouraged by leaders in the church hierarchy even more so than under Marcos. It is more felt and clearly enunciated.

Thus, the church expanded its role to carry out overtly political activity, because it saw this approach as the only way to unite a fragmenting institution. The church not only opposed the Marcos regime but also worked for its collapse. Once Marcos fled the country, the church remained in the political arena to help Aquino's government gain stability. As a result of this experience, the church as an institution shifted more toward the Left. However, once a democratic government was introduced, the church hierarchy tried to shrink the church's role, by reemphasizing its traditional mission and by moving swiftly against the most radical—that is, political—members of the church. Inevitably, though, the church was more involved in politics, and would remain more involved, because of its success in working for political change in establishing the Aquino government.

THE MILITARY AND REGIME CHANGE

While the church was first to come out against the Marcos regime, by the mid-1980s members of the military had begun to quietly lobby for political reform. In the years from 1983 to 1986, this push for political change, organized mostly by RAM, became more extreme. RAM began to call for the need for Marcos either to step down voluntarily or to be overthrown. Prior to Marcos's call for elections, RAM had originally devised a plot to overthrow the government and set up a military junta (Nemenzo 1987, 9; Wurfel 1988, 302; Miranda and Ciron 1988, 11; McCoy 1990, 10). When RAM officers met with General Ver on January 17, 1986, he tried to dissuade them from carrying out any antigovernment activities (Tasker 1986a). RAM officers initially vetoed Ver's request, but the call for elections had caught them by surprise. They decided to postpone the coup attempt and wait to see what the election's outcome would be.

For the 1986 elections, RAM introduced the *Kamalayan* '86 (Consciousness) campaign, to encourage armed forces members to respect the election process (Sacerdoti 1986a, 12). RAM also released a manifesto outlining its position.

It is our basic aim to establish a unique martial tradition for the nation which envisages that in the event we are compelled to intervene in the political life of the nation in order to save it, the Members pledge to each other, that they shall not exercise political power, and that they shall return to their barracks as soon as the sovereign will of the people has prevailed. (Arillo 1986, 164)

During the election, the role of the military was to remain in the barracks, except to vote and to quell terrorist attacks on the ballots. However, the preparations for the elections further split the armed forces. On the one hand, COMELEC deputized the Philippine Constabulary (PC) and the Integrated National Police (INP) to maintain law and order during elections, although they were admonished to stay fifty meters away from the actual polls. Ramos supported COMELEC's requests on both counts, telling his regional commanders to work for "honest, open and peaceful elections" (Tasker 1986a, 26). Officers promised that whatever the outcome, the AFP would support the winner of the election and strictly follow the principle of civilian supremacy (Sacerdoti 1986a, 11; Tasker 1986a, 26).

On the other hand, PC officers and opposition leaders openly feared the behavior of the army, which had traditionally intervened in martial law elections. Members of Ramos's camp, including PC officers and outspoken retired generals, vowed to stop voter intimidation and polling irregularities. One RAM officer said that if there was clear voting fraud, "then we would have to act" (Tasker 1986a, 27). However, Ramos's camp also called for the mass public to protect their ballots.

Fear of military intervention in the elections was bolstered by the COMELEC deputizing the regional unified commanders in Mindanao and the western command to protect the ballots against rebel attacks. However, the opposition claimed that these regions were precisely the ones where they had strong support. Second, a pro-Ver general was moved from his command in the Visayas to one in Central Luzon, where Aquino's home province was located. Third, there were rumors of troops being sent from Mindanao to different areas of the country, including Manila, to form special "election" task forces (Tasker 1986a). Fourth, there were fears that if Aquino were to win the elections, pro-Marcos officers would institute a coup against her. Their incentives would be to ensure that she did not bring Communists into her administration (as Marcos had charged), to reinstate Marcos, and therefore to ensure the continuation of their own power, especially since Aquino had campaigned on retiring overstaying generals (Tasker 1986a).

When the National Assembly declared Marcos the winner of the election, Aquino denounced the vote counting as fraudulent. She called for civil disobedience to force Marcos to give up power and asked Ramos to join her in this effort. However, she was disappointed by his early silence on the issue. She complained that he "is so indecisive. When will he declare what he is for? It may be too late" (Tasker 1986b, 14). However, RAM came out against the election results. On February 16, it released a statement supporting the CBCP's statement, which described the election as fraudulent and called for nonviolent action against the regime. RAM members, speaking off the record, claimed that their younger members—second lieutenants to majors—wanted the organization to act immediately but were being told to be patient (Tasker 1986b).

After the elections, Marcos gave the orders to round up the members of RAM, including Enrile and Ramos (Lande 1986, 143). Enrile and Ramos discovered the arrest orders and decided to revolt against Marcos. They resigned their positions, stating that the 1986 election was fraudulent and that Aquino was the rightful winner. Over two hundred rebel soldiers grouped at Camp Aguinaldo to support them (Bello 1987, 66). The rebels asked Radio Veritas to announce their situation and ask people for help. Cardinal Sin himself came on the radio begging supporters to come to Camp Aguinaldo and to bring provisions for the soldiers (Wurfel 1988, 302). At its peak, the human barricade of people power was estimated at 800,00 (Arillo 1986, 117).

Once the rebels were entrenched in Camp Aguinaldo, Marcos sent loyalist troops there to try to dislodge them and get them to surrender, using force if necessary. Marcos sent tanks, a mortar unit, helicopters, and a transport unit. However, these forces were not successful in ousting the rebels. First, many of the troops whom Marcos ordered to attack the rebels switched sides, refusing to fire. Helicopters and transport units flew to different locations than those ordered, to take their own equipment out of the battle and therefore help the rebels. Military officers continued to communicate with Malacanang Palace as if they were carrying out orders, but they were actually delaying their deployment (Overholt 1986, 1162). Second, the human barricade around the camp deterred the tanks from firing, since they were unwilling to fire into the crowd.

During the events of February 22–25, 1986, Aquino was at first wary of aligning with the rebels, as they were with her. However, as it became clear to RAM that it would not be able to create a military junta, it allied with her, and Aquino overcame her initial suspicions with the group. The agreement forged during these days was that the rebels would support Aquino's presidency (Wurfel 1988, 303). A navy captain, who participated in several coup attempts, said that after the events at EDSA, RAM "wanted six months of transition. We wanted to have a period where you bodily take the country and set it in the right direction. We—RAM and Enrile—asked for two positions— secretary of national defense and chief of staff. The military [pulled back] to let her rule."

While Enrile joined the Aquino government, the rebels were disappointed by this agreement, in general. According to the navy captain, Aquino

was unfaithful to the largely unwritten agreement. . . . Instead of her agreement to give the military a larger role in the government to make changes, regarding cronies, etcetera, there was betrayal. She immediately appointed people, but not from RAM. She made changes too fast. She promised that every cabinet position would be thoroughly discussed with RAM [but they weren't—she'd just announce the appointments]. We felt that she was headed in a separate direction. They [Aquino and her advisors] were afraid of the Enrile group. She threw away the constitution.

They felt that they had caused the collapse of the Marcos regime and his flight to Honolulu. Four informants stated that the military did not want "to go back to the barracks" after the February Revolution because they felt that they had caused the events to happen, they realized how much power they had, and they believed that they could hold onto that power. The military's point of view on the events of 1986 was that "Corazon Aquino may have won the elections, but if the military had not intervened as it did in shifting loyalty from the dictator to Enrile and Ramos, there is serious doubt if she could have effectively claimed the presidency for herself" (Arillo 1986, 126).

However, military members did not feel adequately compensated for this. One general said that some "of us soldiers believed in a coalition government with civilians and military [leaders], under the Freedom Constitution, because of the revolutionary government. . . . So, when they were not consulted, they felt shortchanged."

They tried to remain within the inner circle, through Enrile, to become a power behind the throne. Two outside informants said that the military wanted "a greater role in government, even greater than under Marcos, because they had put Aquino into power." They even felt they should be given "a custodial role in determining political outcomes—like the Indonesia model."

However, one retired navy commander downplayed the interventionist feelings within the AFP after 1986. As he said, the military

felt that they were responsible for the revolution because they could have made it difficult in the country. So they felt they should be recognized. But the military was being downgraded. They were seen as another force to be gotten rid of. Then Aquino released the detainees—the military was against that. . . . But because of the policies at that time, the military was losing against the insurgents. The military [thought it] might wake up surrendering to the insurgents. So, the military sided with Enrile [when he was ousted by Aquino]. This raised suspicions that the military was not professional. People were saying that they should follow the constitution. But the military didn't have any intention of taking over government.

Once Enrile and Ramos were named to positions in the Aquino administration, pressure began to rise to reform the AFP. To that end, Ramos began to overhaul the command structure (Sacerdoti 1986c). RAM members lobbied for the creation of a military court to try officers for self-enrichment during the Marcos years. They especially wanted Marcos loyalists to go on trial to show people that the AFP was improving its image. However, Enrile and Ramos promised that there would be no retribution taken against loyalists, to reunify the institution (Tasker 1986c).

The military felt that the February Revolution had improved their image. To continue this, they coined the phrase New Armed Forces of the Philippines (NAFP) to identify a metamorphosis in both their values and training. They instituted a new counterinsurgency plan, *Mamamayan* (Citizen), which united the goals of national reconciliation, security, and development. Security was redefined "to mean the security of the people, the protection of the citizenry, the protection of the law-abiding components of the population and not the security of Malacanang Palace, not the security of the President's family or the security of a general's family as was practiced in the previous regime" (Ermita 1987, 89). Ramos also promised to reform the AFP, stating that the NAFP would focus its training on values, retire overstaying generals, and raise military salaries (Ramos 1987, 85–86).

In the first sixty days of the Aquino administration, Ramos, as chief of staff, began implementing his reforms. He retired twenty-three out of twenty-nine overstaying generals, including Ver and the commanders of the four services, and in general decreased the number of generals from eighty to fifty-five (Wise 1987, 439; Tasker 1986c; Sacerdoti 1986c). He had officers returned who had been lent to government agencies and corporations; he cut back the size of the Presidential Security Command and reduced it to a ceremonial role; and he reorganized NISA, the intelligence-gathering body (Wise 1987, 440).

There existed a serious risk that Marcos loyalists within the military would not support Aquino, even to the extent of instituting their own coup against her (Sacerdoti 1986c, 40). After the February Revolution, 90 percent of the AFP supported Aquino. However, pro-Marcos splinter groups still existed, especially in Ilocos and Mindanao. Loyalist troops who returned to their units after the election were sent to the provinces for new assignments (Sacerdoti 1986c). However, military officers who had not joined RAM or who were not one of its initial members became disgruntled. They felt that Aquino's policy of national reconciliation, whereby they would be accepted by the AFP as regular members, was not being implemented. Rather, they felt that they were being disproportionately sent out of Manila and to the front to fight the insurgency. On the other hand, the rebels who had supported Enrile and Ramos from the start of the events of 1986 were quickly promoted and given positions in Manila (Selochan 1988, 6).

Thus, the question of the RAM itself became a stumbling point for the reunification of the military. Once the Aquino government was set up, the question arose whether RAM would disband or not. Right after the February Revolution, both Enrile and Navy Captain Rex Robles (a founding member of RAM) suggested that RAM was no longer needed since Marcos had stepped down and since Aquino was introducing reform. Thus, Enrile added that RAM would disband. However, RAM remained organized to act as an advisor to Aquino and to lobby for more reform (Wise 1987, 446–47). By the end of 1986, RAM claimed to have 6,000 members out of the 250,000 members of the AFP. Most of the RAM members were still junior officers who were PMA graduates (RAM to Remain After Undergoing "Redirection" 1986, 1). Enrile and Ramos were thus faced with the task of quieting the RAM. Moderate RAM members suggested that the group take a lower profile so as not to anger leaders and end up ignored (Tasker 1986c).

However, the question of how to control RAM was only a small part of the larger question of military loyalty to the Aquino government. Even Aquino's defense secretary, Enrile, did not support the ratification of the new constitution. He believed that such a ratification would legitimize Aquino's presidency. In fact, 60 percent of the military voted against ratification of the constitution (Hernandez 1988, 230–31). However, once the constitution was ratified, the military agreed to follow and support it (232). Aquino faced eroding support from other factions within the military, as well, for following advisors who leaned toward the Left. She proposed policies that angered RAM: a cease-fire with the NPA; amnesty for NPA human rights violators, but not for the military; and the freeing of all political prisoners, including CPP members (Wurfel 1988, 311; Hernandez 1988, 236). Aquino set up a cease-fire with the NPA to allow for both sides to enter into peace talks. During the cease-fire, the government and the NPA were supposed to negotiate a truce. Aquino further angered the military by naming only civilians to the negotiations panel (Wurfel 1988, 311). First, the AFP argued that a cease-fire with them gave recognition to the Communists and allowed them to play a role in national politics. The CPP used the cease-fire period to improve its public relations. It entered into alliances with leftist political parties to field candidates in the May 1987 elections. Second, the cease-fire allowed CPP officials to travel to Manila openly and campaign for members and review its strategy. Third, while Aquino and other government officials negotiated with the CPP, the AFP was not treated as an equal negotiator. Rather, government officials only kept the AFP informed of those negotiations that were directly related to military affairs (Selochan 1988, 7–8).

While the insurgency problem was the AFP's largest complaint against Aquino, there were others. They felt that Aquino had also expanded the Muslim problem by negotiating and signing an agreement with only one of the several Muslim groups, the MNLF (Selochan 1988, 10). Second, they feared that the reestablishment of the Congress would retain, rather than eradicate, elite politics and cronyism. This could also threaten the return of the politicization of military promotions. Third, perhaps because Aquino comes from a land-owning family, she had not introduced a real land reform program, thereby increasing potential NPA support (11).

The AFP attacked Aquino's policy of appointing local officers-in-charge (OICs) to replace elected local officials whom the government felt were loyal to Marcos. The OIC policy, according to the AFP, increased local hostility levels as old politicians refused to leave and the OICs could not establish their authority (Sacerdoti, 1986d). The AFP also did not support Aquino's creation of a Presidential Human Rights Commission, which was set up to investigate human rights abuse charges against military personnel during the Marcos era. The AFP complained that what they did was no different from what the NPA did, yet NPA members were being released from detention and given amnesty (Wise 1987, 441). Enrile complained that such changes would defeat the purpose of reconciliation and would tie the hands of the military as it went into the field against the insurgents. Aquino's Commission on Good Government, set up to look into corruption during the Marcos years, complained that wealth was stolen not only by the First Family but by AFP members as well (Sacerdoti 1986d). Ramos tried to compromise between the AFP and Aquino by creating an AFP body to investigate such charges of corruption (Anti-Corruption Panel for Philippine Military 1986, 4).

Groups within the military felt that they were as capable as, if not more capable than, the politicians running the country. They also felt that if the military was to overthrow the Aquino government and set up a military government, the country would not immediately rise up to support Aquino but would adopt a wait-and-see approach. They discounted mass support for her administration because of Aquino's inability to solve pressing sociopolitical problems in the country (Selochan 1988, 17). Thus, early in Aquino's administration, the Philippines experienced a string of coup attempts to replace her government.

On July 6–8, 1986, the first coup attempt against Aquino occurred. Arturo Tolentino, Marcos's running mate in the 1986 presidential elections, took over the Manila Hotel and declared Marcos the legitimate president in the Philippines because he had allegedly won the elections. Tolentino released a list of the members of the loyalist cabinet and Enrile's name was on it. Tolentino's revolt, although short-lived and never a serious threat to the government, did have military support. Eleven officers above the rank of lieutenant colonel were involved (Clad 1986a). Military support for the revolt was the result of three grievances against the Aquino government: the commission set up to investigate military human rights abuses under martial law, the cease-fire and negotiations with the CPP/NPA, and the inclusion of left-leaning members (such as Labor Minister Augusto Sanchez, Local Government Minister Aquilino Pimentel, and Executive Secretary Joker Arroyo) in Aquino's cabinet (Clad 1986b, 1986a). Rebel officers were not punished after the event. Ramos ordered them to do a mere thirty push-ups. This solution was seen as the best way toward reconciliation. It was also hoped that such leniency would make rebel soldiers switch their loyalties from Marcos to Enrile and Ramos (Clad 1986a). As a result of the coup, military salaries were raised by 10 percent. Nine colonels were promoted to brigadier general and one navy captain to commodore (Davis 1989, 207).

One clear result of the coup attempt was the strengthening of Enrile's position within the Aquino administration. The coup attempt occurred while Aquino and Ramos were in Mindanao and Laurel was out of Manila. Enrile portrayed himself as the sole actor in ending the coup attempt. It was even suggested that Enrile knew ahead of time that the attempt would occur but allowed it to unfold for three reasons. First, he would be able to identify rebel officers. Second, by offering leniency, he could switch their loyalty to himself. Third, he could allow the coup to send a message to Aquino that the military was not unified behind her and that she must pull back to the Right. Some of Aquino's advisors also suspected Enrile of knowledge of the coup, if not complicity (Clad 1986a).

Enrile came under suspicion again, when a second plot to overthrow the government, on November 21–22, 1986, was discovered by Ramos. This plan was entitled "God Save the Queen." The plan involved RAM officers gaining control of the old National Assembly building, reassembling the old National Assembly members, who were predominantly KBL members, and either naming the former assembly speaker as president or taking power for themselves (Clad 1986c). The coup plot marked a break between Ramos and Enrile. Ramos discovered the plan and quickly sent word for military personnel to ignore orders coming from Enrile. He stated that he personally was supporting the Aquino administration. "The new AFP stands behind the present government of President Aquino, having been elected and installed by the people and whose government is duly recognised by the international community" (11).

Suspected of having planned the coup, Enrile was fired by Aquino on November 23, 1986 (Villegas 1987, 198–99; Clad 1986c). Enrile became the head of the revived Nacionalista party, one of the opposition parties under the Aquino government (Clad 1986c). Aquino also fired leftist members of her cabinet— Pimentel and Sanchez—as a gesture to assuage the military and retain its loyalty (Davis 1989, 207). Rafael Ileto, deputy defense minister, replaced Enrile in the cabinet. Ileto was a professionalist who strictly adhered to the principle of an apolitical armed forces. While he did not believe that the AFP would have instituted a coup prior to 1986, he was worried about the political activities of the Reform the Armed Forces of the Philippines Movement (Tasker 1986d). Ileto met with RAM members after the firing of Enrile and told them that they would now have to prove themselves as professional soldiers, especially for promotion. Subsequently, RAM officers with army commands had armor and heavy weaponry taken away, as a preemptive measure (Tasker 1986e).

Ramos's powers, as chief of staff, were significantly increased after the coup plot (Clad 1986c). In return for his remaining loyal to Aquino rather than siding with Enrile, Ramos also expected Aquino to institute specific reforms that he and the military wanted. On November 15th, Ramos submitted to Aquino a memorandum, signed by himself and the four service chiefs, which specified their demands. The ten points included increased counterinsurgency powers for the AFP, the firing of certain cabinet ministers, the reintroduction of the national security council, the replacement of OICs, and the dismissal of corrupt government officials (Tasker 1986e).

A third coup attempt occurred on January 27, 1987. Military men took over the Channel 7 television station and attempted to take over two military bases and another television station. Aquino agreed to meet with junior officers to listen to their demands. In general, they complained that Aquino still had leftists in her cabinet and that she ignored the advice of military personnel concerning government affairs. In response, Aquino gave the go-ahead to resume fighting with the NPA and to take a hard line against them during the fighting (Davis 1989, 207).

A fourth coup attempt occurred on April 18, 1987. Rebels took over a building in Fort Bonifacio and tried to free rebels who had been detained after the January 27 attempt. In response, Aquino promoted fifty-two officers to colonel or captain (in the navy) for one year and eighty-nine officers to colonel or captain permanently. She also instituted a 15 percent pay raise (Davis 1989, 207, 208).

A fifth coup attempt began on August 28, 1987. Col. Gregorio Honasan, one of the original RAM leaders and a key actor during the February Revolution, led a small group of RAM officers in an attempt to overthrow the Aquino government. During the attempt, rebel officers captured a television station and gained control of the AFP headquarters in Camp Aguinaldo (Clad 1987). Regular army forces had been ordered to retake the headquarters, thus having to fire against the rebels. When they balked, the Philippine Marines were sent in and accomplished the task (Clad and Peterman 1987).

After the August 28 coup attempt, Aquino quickly introduced added reforms to strengthen military loyalty to her administration: pay was raised 60 percent across the board; Aquino changed her cabinet; she endorsed the vigilante groups; and she rejected further negotiations with the CPP/NPA (Clad and Peterman 1987).

In a survey conducted in 1987 of 452 military officers, researchers discovered that "a sizable number of military officers appear to view constitutionalism as a limited commitment, agreeing that in the face of a derelict head of government, any group in the military might unseat him even if this meant resorting to force" (Miranda and Ciron 1988, 15). Furthermore, these officers would consider taking over power themselves, in the short run, to hinder Communist control of the government.

Results from Miranda and Ciron's survey show the military at a crossroads (1988, tables 9, 10, 11, 12). Their belief in themselves as an institution was still strong (92 percent), as was their belief in a continuing Communist threat (71 percent) and in the military's corresponding need for more equipment and manpower to fight the NPA (71 percent). They felt that the government was pro-Left (50 percent) and needed to incorporate the military more into decision making in order to successfully defeat the NPA (57 percent). As an outgrowth of their views concerning the need to defeat the NPA, to be wary of pro-Left government tendencies, and to create a larger role for themselves in insurgency policy, the military also considered the possibility of an increased political role for itself, including taking over the government. They believed that the military's most important role was to protect the government (84 percent) and that military rebels should be punished (50 percent).

The military seemed to be grappling with the question of political rule. Results were split on the question of whether or not the military should take over, even using force, if the head of government was unable to perform properly: 34 percent agreed that the military should act, 33 percent disagreed, and 22 percent said neither. They were more apt to intervene, however, if there was a threat of Communist takeover of the government: 43 percent agreed to intervene, 27 percent disagreed, and 21 percent said neither. They mostly agreed that the military had to improve its image (79 percent), through civic action and socioeconomic projects (86 percent). Yet they also agreed that local government officials were mostly the cause of the rise in the insurgency, through their incompetence (77 percent), thus underscoring the belief that military members themselves were equally if not better suited to run government than politicians and bureaucrats.

The more traditional officers felt that the February Revolution was sui generis. To ensure that it would never happen again, they tried to reinstill the values of civilian supremacy in government and professionalism in the military. Rafael Ileto, defense minister under Aquino, agreed that one of the tasks before the AFP was to reform the military's way of thinking. "Some people, even some high-ranking officers, think that just because they are given a rifle they can tell anybody to do what they want, otherwise they'll use that rifle," he said. "That's the wrong attitude. That's what we are trying to defuse in the minds of our men" (Mydans 1986, 7).

Nine informants said that the events of 1986 were the beginning of the process to return the military to professionalism. The seminars that RAM held before the February Revolution shocked the institution into acting. However, under Aquino, the institution started to change: Aquino retired overstaying generals and the institution changed its goals, focusing on peace and order, civilian supremacy, and the protection of the constitution. Morale rose in response to promotions again being based on performance rather than political loyalty. One informant said that the "military realizes that it cannot live separately from the people. There is a connection between the AFP and the population." Another informant said the "military must be loyal to the flag and to the people." To ensure that this shift from political to professional tasks was successful, the military began a "program of reorientation, to reorient the military according to the Constitution and not in accordance with self-perception." The military focused on addressing the problems of the lack of professionalism, education and training, and reward and punishment. One general said that "because of the power of the gun, the soldier is a potential threat to society. [We] must put the soldiers back in their cage." To do so, he stressed the need to rebuild military loyalty to the constitution and to civilian supremacy.

Five informants were unsure whether or not the military could be successfully reoriented. On the one hand, they admitted that the military must recognize civilian supremacy. It "cannot run a government effectively. It isn't trained. It can only suggest action." On the other hand, they feared that the reforms had not really addressed society's problems, particularly the problem of how to take back the military's advantages under martial law. Concerning the reorientation of the military, two informants said that the "men don't want to accept it. They want what they had before: privilege, income, compensation, honors." Another informant pointed to the coup attempt on August 28 as being a severe setback for the reform process. The "rank and file don't agree with Honasan, but [the] entire military was distrusted. The military has become defensive."

Eight informants said that the power of the military had remained the same or increased since 1986. One retired general said that "1986 loosened the military from democratic moorings. [We] took sides in issues in which we shouldn't have taken sides." Three informants said that civilians depend on the military now, and that as a result the military is "more powerful in politics now than they ever were under Marcos." An air force colonel said that "there has been a permanent change [between civil-military relations]." Two informants said that Aquino is too weak to control the military, and so the institution has sensed this and worked it to its advantage. As an example, one outside informant mentioned the event at Mendiola Bridge, where the military fired into a demonstration led by human rights activists. Another informant said that the military felt ignored under Aquino and used the backlash against leftist members of her cabinet to increase their own power. One general blamed the continuing politicization of the military on the RAM. "Most of the military wants to be professional, but the RAM loyalists are aggrieved— they feel they can do better."

Six informants said that the military is highly fragmented as a result of 1986. "The military is still fractionalized. This is the reason why Aquino is still there. When one faction moves, another takes a countermove. But their demands are identical: increase the military budget, increase salaries, [institute a] comprehensive counterinsurgency program (i.e., to expand their [own] political authority)."

On one side are the older officers, who want a return to professionalism. They want the military to be completely under civilian supremacy and acting only according to constitutional authority. "We who are still in the military who come from the old school have clamped down on [politics in the military]. This is not right. We must follow the chain of command. . . . We have been able to impress on the rank and file that we have to go back to basics."

On the other side are the younger officers, who believe that "regardless of the constitution, the armed forces have the right to intervene in politics, especially in the reestablishment of civilian institutions." They have supported Honasan in his coup attempts.

Thus, the military adopted a political role, ousting the Marcos regime. When the Aquino government was created, groups within the military believed that they should stay in the political arena, because they wanted to work to ensure reform and because they felt that Aquino owed them a power-sharing role. While the institution as a whole accepted its role during the February Revolution, the generals believed that the military should return to its professional role and leave politics to the politicians. As political officers revolted against the Aquino administration, the institution prosecuted them more severely, to underline their determination that the military must obey civilian supremacy. Like the church, then, the military adopted and retained its political role because of its experience under the Marcos regime, its effort to overthrow the regime, and its help in installing Aquino to power.

CONCLUSION

The experiences of the church and the military were often parallel during the events of 1986. The members of the hierarchy in both institutions finally agreed to adopt a political role and overthrow the Marcos regime because they saw this position as the only way to reunify their institutions. Once the Aquino government was set up, however, this fragmentation continued, as the hierarchies tried to move the institutions back toward their traditional positions, while rank-and-file groups wanted to remain in the political arena. As a result, conflict within the institutions continued and caused political instability.

7 The Aftermath of Regime Change in the Philippines

INTRODUCTION

■ Initially, both the church and the military saw the events of 1986 as rejuvenating. Both institutions felt that they had come closer to their ideal roles of serving the people. Both felt self-congratulatory jubilation in participating to overthrow the Marcos regime. Once Aquino's government was installed, the mood became less celebratory. The hierarchies of both institutions saw this period as an opportunity to reassert their control. To this end, the leaders of both the church and the military pushed for the depoliticization of their institutions. However, the rank and file in both institutions felt that such a move was a retreat and they fought the retrenchment. These lower groups did not trust their leaders to continue to push for reform. Thus, after 1986, both institutions became even more fragmented as the rank and file fought to remain involved in politics while the hierarchies tried to pull out of the political arena.

THE EFFECT OF POLITICAL ACTIVITY ON THE CHURCH

After the February Revolution, the initial church position was to support and help the Aquino administration. However, by 1987, the church's position began to change in two ways. First, the church began to retreat from direct political involvement. It decided to revert to its original indirect role, by influencing lay people who would then act directly in politics. Second, it began to criticize the Aquino government for reneging on campaign promises and failing to institute needed socioeconomic reform.

A survey was conducted in late 1987 of the membership of the Bishops-Businessmen's Conference. One question concerned whether the respondent felt that the situation in his or her area of the country was the same, better, or worse than two years before. Businessmen in Manila were more optimistic about the business environment, employment, and the economic condition of people in general. Bishops and religious leaders outside of Manila were pessimistic on these same three topics, but more optimistic on government performance (such as the delivery of public services, and graft and corruption) and the level of violence (such as crime level, insurgency level, taxation/liquidations by the NPA, abuses by the military, and abuses by paramilitary vigilantes) (Carroll 1988, 2).

The results offered support for conservative church members who believed that the Aquino government was improving the socioeconomic condition and that therefore, the church could return to its traditional role. However, the survey also offered evidence for the rank and file in that, while some advancement had been made, reforms were still needed, particularly in the rural areas.

Once the Aquino government was installed, the church was divided as to what exactly it should do: if it should only exert influence indirectly or if it should act openly. Cardinal Sin stated that after 1986, the church should withdraw from direct political activity (Tasker 1987). While the church hierarchy wanted retrenchment, the AMRSP felt that the church must continue to work in the political arena. "While we have entered a new time with a greater sense of democratic space and renewed hope, we are only too aware that many obstacles to full liberation remain" (AMRSP 1986).

They believed that, while political change had been achieved, economic change would not be forthcoming without strong church participation. In their mission statement after the events of 1986, they called for socioeconomic reform, specifically mentioning the need

to safeguard national sovereignty, to promote democratic processes at all levels, to actively pursue peace-building and national reconciliation based on justice, to promote education based on nationalist values, to call attention to protect and preserve our ecological systems, to foster economic self-reliance through genuine land reform, agricultural and industrial development programs in consonance with our national aspirations so that we may stand dignified and equal among the family of nations. (AMRSP 1986)

The statement underscored the prophetic role of the church. It stated clearly that in order to achieve these goals, the church must play an active role. "To meet these challenges, we must be open to start new initiatives, actively participate in programs of others and to promote the building of ecclesial communities, people's organizations and consultative bodies especially among the poor, because we see in them a potent force for nation building" (AMRSP 1986).

After the coup attempts, the church hierarchy realized that Aquino needed its help to maintain her moderate position and not move to the right as a result of military pressure (Tasker 1987). In 1989, the bishops of Manila released a pastoral letter, which stated that under "the circumstances obtaining in our country today, the staging of a coup-d'etat, which is in violation of our Constitution is an unlawful usurpation of power; it is a rebellion not only against duly constituted authority but against God from whom all civil authority is derived" (Constantino 1990).

However, church support for Aquino's government translated into neither support for her specific policies nor reunification of the church itself. Thus, after the events of 1986, the church adopted a position of "constructive critical solidarity" (Youngblood 1989, 68–69). Even as it supported her, the church began to voice concerns over the continued crony politics, human rights abuses, and the administration's policy vis-à-vis the insurgency. When the Aquino administration began its negotiations with the CPP/NPA for a cease-fire, the church was supportive and church officials served on the National Cease-Fire Committee (5). When the cease-fire discussions collapsed, Aquino moved to take strong military action against the NPA. As a result, criticism of the Aquino administration and disagreement within the church mounted. Cardinal Sin came out in agreement with Aquino's policy that military force was now called for. Conservative bishops sided with him. On the other hand, Bishop Labayan denounced Aquino's policy as going directly against Gospel doctrine of antiviolence (5). Church officials who were closer to the poor felt that the administration had tricked the church. They believed that Aquino had never been serious in her cease-fire approach. Rather, she was looking for an excuse to fight an all-out war with the NPA (7).

Thus, the church as an institution became more defensive, particularly concerning charges of leftist infiltration of the church (Youngblood 1989, 4), especially since the administration's renewed conflict with the CPP/NPA refocused attention on this question. Bishop Claver stated that now that Marcos was gone and Aquino in power, the church could move against its more leftist members. "Before, to finger a priest who was working with the Left would mean his arrest under the Marcos regime" (Tasker 1987, 17). In 1987, the church also released a pastoral letter, "The Fruit of Justice is Peace," which further condemned church organizations (and their members) that advocated violence (Youngblood 1989, 11n.20). These charges of infiltration and responding defensiveness further fragmented the church.

For years, NASSA (the National Secretariat for Social Action) had been one of the most outspoken organs of the church. As the social action arm of the CBCP, it took early and aggressive positions on Marcos's regime and his policies. In 1987, the CBCP became suspicious that NASSA was becoming too independent. In particular, the bishops feared that the organization was infiltrated by leftists, conducting pro-Left programs, and was channeling funds to the National Democratic Front. The CBCP's committee to investigate NASSA programs and policies found its work made more difficult as NASSA officials refused to explain where and on what its funds were being spent. The committee's report eventually exonerated NASSA (Youngblood 1989, 9–10). However, in 1988, NASSA was brought more closely under the control of the bishops. The national director and the board of trustees were replaced and decision making was centralized. By taking this action, the bishops implied that they now believed that there were Communist members in their organizations, that they did not support such members' political activity, and that they would no longer protect them (Sin 1988, 27). However, this position taken by Sin was strongly condemned by other bishops because it went against the committee's generally favorable report.

When asked whether or not they thought that the church would be involved in political tasks in the future, four informants took a noninterventionist position. As one Jesuit priest said, "as political stability is achieved by the Aquino administration, as it achieves a better distribution of income and a better human rights situation, the church can and should stay in the level of ideas and principles."

Another informant, a member of the church hierarchy, also mentioned the return to democracy as a rationale for the church's returning to its traditional role. He said that the laity should take over and that the church should only act indirectly, through influencing the laity. Two informants said that the church must now be cautious, because if "we interfere, then neoclericalism becomes anticlericalism." One bishop said that while the church must speak up for morality and justice, it "should never be involved in partisan politics."

When asked whether they personally thought that the church should play more of a role or less of a role in politics, seven informants mentioned that they thought it should play less of one. As one Jesuit priest said, when "the values of society are in crisis, no institution can be neutral. But when it is a question not of basic values, but of how policies should be implemented, then the church should let people form their own opinions."

Three informants said that the church should get out of the political sphere and let the laity and the politicians fill those roles. Two informants pointed out particular costs for the church if it were to remain filling a political role. One Jesuit said that political "activity is not an area where the church should get involved, especially partisan politics, because the church is for everyone. If the church takes sides in partisan politics where moral issues are not clear, it would be defeating its own mandate to be for all people. That is a sure way of alienating people."

A leftist bishop said that the church would only return to the political arena depending on the political situation, since it "responds upon the plight of the people."

Eight informants mentioned that the church will act disparately, with some groups pulling out while other groups remain involved in politics. The most optimistic informant in this group, a religious superior, said that she hoped that the church would allow as legitimate behavior a "diversity of approaches." Two informants made general distinctions between who would be active in the future and who would not. One priest said that because most of the church members are "comfortable," most of them will not be involved in the future because they fear a threat to their situations. The other informant, a sister, said that the popular church will continue to reflect on the conditions of the people because it "is with the people." Three informants specified the particular paths groups within the church would take. They said that the CBCP would be less involved, while the AMRSP would remain in the political sphere. Regarding the hierarchy, one sister complained that the

majority in the church will tend to go back to the traditional way of doing things—because they are more comfortable. [They will] try to preserve the traditional way. In 1986–1988, many church members saw the problems under Marcos resolved: there was a new president, new changes. There was a sense that the church had done its duty, had brought about change. So, the church could go back to its practice, to the more conservative stream: spiritual emphases, as if this is separate from [the] material, earthly concerns of man.

Regarding the popular church, one priest said that it would be more involved in the future. "That is the direction of the people's church. The church is not in the periphery but in the midst of the political world. Not as kingmakers, but to translate into concrete terms what it means to be of the . . . church. Because it will be more and more involved in the political life of the people."

One sister said that members of this church were learning from the Nicaraguan experience that church involvement must occur carefully so as not to introduce change too fast. The church "must respect the people's forms of faith (rituals) because that is what they understand." As a result, the popular church has accepted that they are undertaking a long-term commitment.

However, there is the sense that, whether or not the church directly remains in political affairs in the future, the institution's role has changed permanently—that the political role has become a permanent part of its self-image. Three informants said that all things being equal, the church would not reenter politics. However, they also all agreed that if the current political situation deteriorated—if "the government deteriorates," if "things become so bad again," if "there is a need for the church to lead"— then the church would become politically involved again.

Twelve informants admitted that whether the church liked it or not, it would remain involved: less involved in politics perhaps, but more involved in social change. Of these twelve, nine mentioned moderate reasons, such as church involvement being integral to its ecclesiastical role. A brother said that "since being involved in social change would mean entanglements to politicians and politics as well, I'm afraid the church will be very much involved, although not with partisan politics." Four mentioned that the "church will always look at moral dimensions, so it will always be involved," specifically in justice issues, BCCs, and influencing lay people. A Jesuit pointed to the pope's own statements as a rationale for the church's involvement. A sister said that the church "should be more involved with people, so that they will be able to find alternative ways, to participate, to preserve their own dignity by learning how to take care of one another and living [in] Basic Christian Communities." The lay worker cautioned, though, that while the church may remain involved, it "has to find its own kind of role and rhythm. The problem is that people always want to say, 'let's do it again,' but that doesn't work. Time changes, mood changes. The church hasn't found the right mix yet, what today's church and people feel is [the] right mix. The church will go searching [for the answer] for several years."

Of these twelve, seven informants mentioned more sociopolitical reasons for church involvement in politics in the future. One Jesuit said that it would be more involved in the future because the church's "mission would not be complete if it could not contribute to a just socioeconomic-political order." A sister said that they would "still carry on with the goal of social transformation." Another sister specified that the church must find a way to anchor work for "human rights and social justice—in our own ministries. We may not be as visible as before, but we are still involved." Four informants pointed to the inevitability of continued church involvement.

As long as the social crisis is unresolved, there is more poverty, the church will be more involved. The masses are still passive. The priest has to play a political role, to lead his community. Because we still have an undifferentiated society. There are no intelligentsia in the communities. When society is more differentiated, when there are more intelligentsia, when the masses are more active, then the religious will play a less prominent role. But this may take 20–30 years.

A religious superior said that political organizations

are not that strong in the Philippines. People here look for institutions or people to champion their needs for them with the government. So, the church is still looked up to. So, it will depend on the rapidity of how fast public institutions can articulate people's needs. The church is seen as an important conduit for getting certain concerns addressed. As long as so many Philippine people are so poor, they are vulnerable. They can be intimidated easily by the mayor or the police. The priest is the only one who can seriously do it without the fear of being mauled.

Two informants said that it was inevitable for the church to remain in the political arena because there was a leadership vacuum in the country. They argued that there were serious flaws in Aquino's ability to run the government. As a result, the church would be forced to remain in the political arena to aid her administration or to influence her policies to ensure reform, because there did not "seem to be any improvement in the national situation" and because "the tendency of the powers that be is to suppress people or terrorize them."

When asked what they personally believed, six informants said that the church would play more of a role in politics because it responds to the people. Two said that its concern for social questions would lead it into more involvement "because as a leadership body it has to make a stand on issues which people can rally behind and trust." One said that the church had to become more involved in order to remain relevant to the lives of people, "otherwise the church will go the way of the dinosaurs." One priest put it more forcefully. "The church must rejoin history, it must rejoin the human race. If it has no contact with people in the daily life, it is not a church—it is just an institution. [The problem] is quite serious. People may join idealistic groups instead."

One sister said that since the church has educated the people in how to participate, it "cannot just leave the people." A cardinal said that the "moment I keep quiet, the people say . . . 'speak.' So I am forced to speak. Because my people demand that I interfere. . . . The moment we do not [do] those things, who will say it? Is it interference? No, it is my job."

Six informants mentioned that a political role was an integral part of the church's work. One priest said that one

can't avoid the moral issues or separate it from [the] political. The church has to take a stand. During martial law even if it had lost everything, at least people would see. But under martial law, the church wanted both—it wanted to keep churchgoers and complain about the regime simultaneously. So it ended up not making a very strong stand. It would have been better if the church had taken a strong stand, even if it lost everything. At least then people would know what the church stood for.

Another priest said that it "is the role of the church in the world, its mission mandate to proclaim the kingdom. Christians are called to work for social transformation. It is its mandate to influence social order, to influence social and political realities, to support Christian values. The institutional church is not nearly as involved as it should be." A sister specified that she chose to work in a political ministry because she felt that preaching "the good news involved politics in a broad sense, not partisan politics." A priest said that "people have gotten tired of sermons and pure talk. They want a church that does something—to not just address the symptoms but alleviate causes." A lay worker said that church involvement is a pure ministry because it is unselfish: when "bishops, priests get involved in this work, they're at their best."

Seven informants said that the church should play more of a role in politics in the future because of societal conditions. They stressed the link between how social structures are set up and the level of injustice in the country.

When we talk about helping the poor, making the kingdom visible and alive, we are talking about 70 percent of the population. So we must go into human rights—housing, health, land distribution. Evangelization has to happen in the real situation. We have to organize BECs. We have to organize our own people because they don't know how to work things out. The elites and rich won't give up their rights. We have democracy now, so we have to use it to organize people.

A priest said that he would

like the church to be more involved in the basic issues of the country, sociopolitical issues. The church should be more serious again in socio-cultural issues. The country has been sold to the colonizer. It has been molded to serve the interests of the elite. The church in the past has been a willing ally to the betrayal of the Filipino culture. The new church will be involved in retrieving Filipino culture. Who else will do that?

One sister said that the Philippine church should learn from the Nicaraguan church how to "be more prophetic, take the side of the poor."

One priest said that the church must play a role in the new political situation in the country. "We are facing a national crisis. The church has the resources, the symbolic capital, the credibility for national reconstruction and liberation. The church today is heavily involved in more secular choices." Regardless of the country's return to democracy, one informant said that church members "have to remain vigilant, no matter what the regime is, for transformation toward justice, peace, democracy."

Three said that the church should become more involved, but that it would further fragment the institution. One sister said,

[structural] analysis is so very important. We must know what is going on. Reflection is needed. Not just "action-action." Others see me as progressive but I consider myself a moderate. I tell the progressive sisters to slow down and let the traditional sisters catch up. I can see the value in the traditional sisters' approach. [But] faith cannot just be kept inside the four walls of a convent. We must live it.

Thus, while some members wanted the church to withdraw, most realized that it was not possible to return to a purely conservative position. On the other side, a group within the institution wanted it to take an even more activist stance, to gain reforms that had not materialized under the Aquino administration.

THE EFFECT OF POLITICAL ACTIVITY ON THE MILITARY

After the February Revolution, the military initially fully supported Aquino's administration. However, by 1987, this support began to crumble. On the one hand, the professionals were placed in control of the military. They saw as their primary duty the reorganization of the military and its depoliticization. On the other hand, military officers who had played an active role in the February Revolution complained that Aquino was breaking her agreement to share power informally with the military and that she was not introducing economic and political reforms. The resulting fragmentation within the military caused the professionals to push Aquino for more power and resources for the institution while it caused the politicos to institute numerous coup attempts against Aquino.

Those who wanted a reprofessionalization of the military identified three general areas in which reform was needed. First, the military would have to focus on the training of personnel, to increase discipline and return to military traditions, such as chain of command and accountability. Military abuses needed to be identified and military personnel punished if found guilty. The military also needed to redefine its role in strictly military concerns. Thus, they wanted the military to focus on defending the country and the constitution rather than the president and the regime (Hernandez 1987, 237–39).

Second, they wanted the AFP to be reunified. They sensed that fraternal organizations threatened the military man's loyalty to the president and the constitution because they inserted another person or group between himself and his country. Thus, while such groups as RAM were helpful in overthrowing the

Marcos regime and were also pushing for reform, they must be downgraded within the AFP (Hernandez 1987, 239).

Outside observers added a third requirement to achieve reprofessionalization: the separation of the AFP from foreign influence. Because of the existence of American bases and the Joint United States Military Advisory Group (JUSMAG), they feared that the AFP risked being influenced more by external interests than internal ones. Specifically, American influence may have forced the Philippines to focus on the insurgency rather than other problems. Thus, the AFP, as well as the Philippines, needed to become self-reliant and independent (Hernandez 1987, 241).

The professionals saw military reorganization as achieving three goals. First, it would purge the institution of politicized personnel whose loyalty was suspect. Second, it would improve civil-military relations by reassuring the mass public that the military was no longer the oppressive arm it had been under martial law.

Third, it would show Aquino not only that it was loyal but also that her administration depended on it. In 1987, Ramos pointed out to Aquino several groups across the political spectrum as working for her overthrow. His discussion pointed out that the Aquino government was not secure from threat. The indirect point was that it was secure only to the extent that the military supported it. Therefore, the military believed it had significant leverage to gain concessions from Aquino. Ramos claimed that the CPP-NPA had drafted a six-year plan, beginning in 1986 and running concurrently with Aquino's term. This plan stressed infiltration of the government through three stages, rather than armed revolt. Stage one involved CPP/NPA and NDF individuals gaining positions in Aquino's administration. Stage two involved these individuals rising to sensitive positions in government. Stage three involved the NDF getting a member selected as a presidential candidate for 1992 (Pimentel 1987, 13).

The Mindanao secessionists posed the second threat. While

this threat was not described as being as serious as the first one, it did have the problem of fragmentation. The Muslims were broken into three groups: the Moro National Liberation Front (with 19,800 men), the Moro Islamic Liberation Front (with 3,300 men), and the MNLF-Reformist Group (with 540 men). While this threat was not as large as the CPP/NPA, it had the problem of being so fragmented that it was hard to negotiate with them to end the war (Pimentel 1987, 13–14). The last group was composed of the ultrarightists, a loose coalition of several diverse groups. These groups include Marcos supporters, Honasan followers within the military, and individuals who would themselves like to run the country. Ramos claimed that Marcos and Honasan forces were merging to overthrow the government and set up a civilian-military junta (14).

However, the most serious threat to Aquino's administration came from ex–RAM members themselves. After the August 28, 1987, coup attempt, the Aquino government felt that it was important to quell the threat of another coup attempt. First, it took a hard line against the rebels. In contrast to her previous policies regarding rebels, Aquino stated that the rebels should surrender, that there would be no terms negotiated regarding their surrender, and that they would be punished as mutineers under the Articles of War (The Laurel Report 1987, 1).

PMA cadets were surprised that the Aquino government punished the rebels. They wondered why rebels were rewarded in 1986, during the events of EDSA, but reviled in 1987 (Bernas 1988, 7). One advisor to the president implied that the events of 1986 created an agreement between the government and the military. The former agreed to be both "legitimate and credible," while the latter promised to return to professionalism. Thus, it was warned that Aquino "should not easily presume that the civilian supremacy formula of the Constitution will protect [her] from a fate similar to that of the civilian Mr. Marcos" (7). One PMA cadet who had supported the rebels stated, after the coup was over, that he felt he had done "the right thing," modifying this statement only to say that while the methods may have been wrong, the cause was correct (Walsh 1988, 3).

Aquino's second initiative in response to the August 28, 1987, coup attempt was to direct Vice President Laurel to conduct a survey of military personnel to discover why the coup occurred and how future attempts could be prevented. In particular, the survey was designed to see whether or not the perceived reasons for the coup were correct. These reasons included alleged government favoring of the Communists while dealing harshly with the military, alleged Communist sympathizers holding high office in Aquino's administration, and low wages and poor equipment for the AFP (The Laurel Report 1987, 1).

The survey was conducted with almost six thousand officers and enlisted men in both the AFP and the INP nationally (The Laurel Report 1987, 1). The results pointed out both military dissatisfaction with government performance and differences within the military in the magnitude of dissatisfaction felt.

1. Concerning conditions in the AFP, less than 50 percent of the senior officers, 73 percent of the field grade and junior officers, and 62.8 percent of the noncoms and enlisted men were unhappy with conditions.
2. Concerning salaries, almost 80 percent of the senior officers and 95 percent of all other respondents considered their salary to be low.
3. Concerning alleged Communist infiltration of the Aquino government, 64 percent of the senior officers and 73.6 percent of the field grade officers agreed that it existed. Asked whether or not they felt that the government favored Communists, about half of both senior officers and field grade officers agreed.
4. Concerning Honasan's behavior, 95 percent of the senior officers and 70 percent of the field grade officers disapproved of his actions. However, 53.8 percent of the junior

grade officers and 56.6 percent of the noncoms and enlisted men approved of his actions. Similarly, 75 percent of the senior officers and 41.5 percent of the field grade officers believed that he should be court-martialed, while 53.6 percent of the junior officers and 75.8 percent of the noncoms and enlisted men felt that he should be pardoned.

5. Concerning the cabinet, 50.8 percent of the senior officers, 59.5 percent of the field grade officers, 66.3 percent of the junior officers, and 58.2 percent of the noncoms and enlisted men felt that it should be revamped.

6. Concerning the AFP chief of staff, 7.7 percent of the senior officers, 12.6 percent of the field grade officers, 17.7 percent of the junior officers, and 12.3 percent of noncoms and enlisted men judged him to be weak. (The Laurel Report 1987, 1–2)

Several general observations were also made by the researchers during informal discussions after the questionnaires had been filled out. The soldiers aired concerns such as: the government does not care about them, the Presidential Commission on Human Rights hampers their anti-insurgency campaigns, the release of detained Communist leaders hinders the military's task to end insurgency, the government's policy of a cease-fire favors the Communists while thwarting the military, the government has a double standard because it is lenient with the Communists but harsh with the coup rebels, the OICs whom Aquino appointed worsen the insurgency situation, and religious groups and individuals overtly support the CPP/NPA (The Laurel Report 1987, 2).

As a result, Aquino began to move away from the Left and toward the military, that is, toward the Right. When Aquino began her presidency, she promised to work for human rights, for the poor and the underprivileged, for the rule of law, national reconciliation, and nationalist policies (Constantino 1988, 19). However, by late 1987, Aquino began to back away from this agenda. Police raids in Manila were conducted without arrest warrants and vigilante groups were encouraged to form (20).

On April 2, 1988, Honasan, the leader of the August 1987 coup attempt, and the thirteen men who were to guard him during detention escaped from a navy ship anchored in Manila Bay. Eleven of the original coup leaders and ninety enlisted men had not returned to their barracks almost a year after the coup attempt (Mydans 1988a, 3). There were immediate fears of another coup attempt. Aquino threatened that severe action, including court-martial, would be taken against Honasan if he were caught.

However, Honasan had several well-wishers within the AFP who were happy that he was able to escape. Soldiers referred to the pay raise Aquino gave them after the August coup attempt as the "Honasan bonus." Thus, despite Aquino's reforms, soldiers still agreed with the RAM's position that Aquino neither cared about the military nor knew how to lead it (Mydans 1988b).

A mass public survey was conducted in Manila on April 12–13, 1988. 48 percent of those surveyed said that they thought Honasan had the ability to launch another coup. 62 percent said it was the duty of citizens to help the government capture Honasan. 49 percent believed that the AFP could be depended on to capture Honasan. Only 32 percent thought that Honasan was a credible leader because his interests were for the good of the country. Only 36 percent felt that more than half of the military would support Honasan, although 68 percent believed that he could not have escaped without help from high-level military officials and 63 percent believed he had politicians as accomplices in order to escape. Overall, 4 percent said their opinion of Honasan had gone up, 55 percent said it remained the same, and 39 percent said it was worse. In separate surveys, in September 1987, 63 percent were dissatisfied, and in October 1987, 56 percent were dissatisfied with Honasan (Social Weather Stations 1988).

In 1988, twenty-one army officers were promoted to the rank of general even though most of them were to retire within several months. This unusual promotion pattern was due to Ramos's targeting of officers who had been denied promotion under martial law because of generals who stayed on under Marcos as a reward for their loyalty to the First Family. Ramos believed that promoting these officers was a way both to make up for the wrong done to them under martial law and at the same time to strengthen the army's loyalty to Ramos and Aquino. This second reason was particularly important given the recent coup attempts. Ramos wanted to use this loyalty to get promises from the government that its anti-Communist policy would become tougher. In particular, Ramos wanted three reforms passed by Congress: the death penalty, a national identity card, and a citizens' army (General Rejoicing 1988, 26).

Ileto resigned as defense minister in January 1988 because of this policy of promotion as well as other ministry policies. Ileto felt that such promotions meant that the new generals would "spend a few months settling in, then a few more operating at 50 percent efficiency, and their last months looking for a nice civilian job." Furthermore, Ileto charged the military, especially Ramos, with ignoring his plans to reorganize and reform the AFP (General Rejoicing 1988, 26).

The most serious threat to Aquino's regime was the coup attempt on December 1, 1989. The coup followed a drop in Aquino's popularity to below 50 percent (Timberman 1990, 168). Both opponents and defenders of the Aquino administration had been complaining about her mishandling of the Communist insurgency, the mounting corruption charges against Aquino's own family members, and her general lack of leadership on pressing social problems (Coronel 1989b). Furthermore, it was generally agreed that the timing of the coup attempt was planned to take advantage of nagging complaints regarding Aquino's lack of leadership in the economic arena. Indeed, opposition became so heated after the coup that several critics argued that a strong (i.e., authoritarian) leader would be preferable, as long as he or she delivered reform (Sanger 1989a).

The Philippine government admitted that the coup attempt

was supported by a diverse group, including generals, business-men, opposition leaders, and Marcos supporters, and that it had wealthy financial backing (Pear 1989; Manila Describes Evidence on Plot 1989, 3). It was the result of RAM and pro-Marcos groups entering into an alliance. Because of this alliance, the mass public was not lobbied for support; rather, RAM targeted the AFP for its support, while the Marcos loyalists provided financial aid (McBeth 1989). Over three thousand rebel soldiers led by the group of RAM officers involved in the events of 1986 and two of the previous five coup attempts fought for control of several military bases, including Camp Aguinaldo, Villamor Air Base, and Mactan Air Base (on the island of Cebu). The battle for Camp Aguinaldo was both strategic and symbolic, since it was not only army headquarters but also the location of the February Revolution. The rebels also took over the center of Manila's fi-nancial district, Makati, where they occupied government build-ings, business offices, residential areas, and luxury hotels (Coronel 1989a; Timberman 1990, 176). The United States al-lowed two U.S. Air Force planes to pin down the rebels' airplanes without actually firing at the planes or the rebels. This aid was crucial in giving the loyalists the advantage they needed to attack the rebel positions (Coronel 1989a, 1989b). Rebel forces began to withdraw from the three military bases they occupied and from two television stations. After several days of negotiations, the rebels also surrendered their positions in Makati. They re-turned to their barracks without having to surrender their weap-ons (Timberman 1990, 176).

The events after the December 1989 coup attempt pointed out that while American military assistance protected the Aquino government from collapse, it could not stop criticism of her ad-ministration from continuing to mount or confidence in her ad-ministration from continuing to fall. Right after the coup attempt, the Philippine stock market dropped 20 percent (Sanger 1989b). More serious was the fact that rumors of new coup at-tempts continued to arise (Pear 1989).

After the 1989 coup attempt, military officers loyal to Aquino tried to quickly adopt new reforms, especially to reindoctrinate soldiers and to check on the loyalty of officers. "According to most accounts, officers and men from [former Scout Ranger Chief Brig. Gen. Marcelo] Blando's 71st and 73rd battalions were duped into thinking they were reinforcing government units, and the majority of them deserted when they were engaged by loyal Marines" (McBeth 1989, 19).

When asked whether they thought that the military would be involved in political tasks in the future, nine informants said that they thought that the military would play less of a role or no role. Of these nine, seven said that this would be due to the military itself. Several reasons given included the belief that the RAM would disappear, that the number of disgruntled soldiers was small, that the institution would be successfully depoliticized, that reforms would be introduced, that the Philippine soldier was not inclined to be involved in politics, and that the military would be united. One general said that

[We] will go back [to the old military]. We will visit units, strengthen the line of command, hold seminars, and punish those who continue to follow the same thing. What made this group of Honasan's credible was that their demands, purposes, grievances are really legitimate: low pay, lack of uniforms, corruption. Their demands are true. We have to explain—you cannot get these things [reforms] by going out directly to politicians, by using arms to get them. After Honasan, salaries have increased 60–90 percent—90 percent for lower ranks, 60 percent for higher ranks.

Another general agreed, saying that the soldiers "will go back in the cage. Only the highly politicized people, who are not the representatives of the soldiers, will not be there" inside the cage.

Another informant said that the younger officers understood that the military had to become depoliticized if the government was to work and that continuing politicization would cause a return to authoritarianism in the long run.

Of the nine informants, two felt that the military's change would be due to the Aquino government. One informant mentioned that the military's role would naturally decline as the government became stronger. The other two informants mentioned Aquino herself: that she did not want the military involved in politics, so she would not place them in civilian positions. Also,

Aquino has the loyalty of more and more military men because she gave due recognition to the military. She has been visiting camps, increasing the pay and allowances of soldiers. She is beginning to attend to the welfare of the military. She has more military support now than after the February Revolution. Most of the generals now (particularly the field commanders) were appointed by her, since the revolution.

Fifteen informants said it was too close to predict whether the military would be more or less involved in the future. Four said it depended on Aquino: the military will not be involved if she supports democracy, if she can control the military, if she does not give them political tasks, and if she can crush coup attempts. A newspaper editor pointed out that some military officers "will intervene if they have a chance. Most of them are realizing that the civilians have authority. . . . The more the [Aquino] government has demonstrated that it could crush [coup] attempts, the less that future attempts will be tried."

Three said military withdrawal from politics depended on leaders in general: if they use the military for political ends and if they can govern effectively. One general said that it depends "on how the political leaders run the country. If they run it properly, if there is good government, then the military will keep to its role. If it doesn't, history [in the Philippines] and the experience of other countries show that the military will take it upon themselves to intervene in the political environment of the country."

Four informants said it depended on the insurgency. Two of the four said that if leftists and Communists tried to take over the government, then the military would intervene. Two informants said it depended on conditions in the country in general.

Two informants said that it "depends on the situation—insurgency, corruption, government performance, legitimacy. That's what made the military act against Marcos." Another said that the "Philippines will be like Spain—it took them five years to unite the military." Two informants said that whether or not the military withdrew from politics depended on whether or not the government could fulfill the needs of the country. A navy captain said that if "the civilian government fails to do its job, then it is a natural reaction for the military to become more involved."

Thirteen informants said that they thought that the military would become more involved in the political sphere in the future. One said that this was due to the government: that Aquino has to rely on the military. Three said that it was due to the conditions in the country: the Left was becoming stronger, there was still civil disorder in the country, and there was no improvement in socioeconomic conditions. One general said that "if the military feels that the leaders are slowly losing the country to the Communists, then that is a strong argument in favor of having the military take a role. There are many models—many Asian countries with dictatorships."

Three of these thirteen informants said that the military would be involved, but they were optimistic: one said that only retired officers would be involved, by running for office, while another said that although the military will always be politicized, it would not intervene. However, three informants were more pessimistic. They believed that the military would intervene in the future, because many military officers still believed that they could do a better job than the civilians, because morale was still low, and because they had been politicized under martial law. One journalist said that the threat of military intervention was greater now. The military "are more insidious now. There is a more crafty projection of its real power." Another outside informant said that the "moment you give soldiers experience in politics, you cannot get them back out of politics. This is the permanent legacy of Marcos. Once politicized, they cannot be depoliti-cized."

A retired general said that it "will be very difficult to divorce [the military from politics] now. Before, the military was seen as a killing machine. Now, that machine thinks."

Three informants made the argument that the military would have to intervene, and that such intervention was natural, because the country is underdeveloped and had just undergone a regime change. Another said that officers were studying Latin America because the Philippines is more similar to it than to its Asian neighbors. They were focusing in particular on political events in Argentina, Bolivia, the Dominican Republic, El Salvador, Guate-mala, Haiti, Honduras, Nicaragua, Uruguay, and Peru.

One retired general pointed out that the choice of intervention versus withdrawal would be influenced by whether or not the military sensed that there was a leadership vacuum. Thus, the role that the military plays in the future will depend in large part on the behavior of the new government itself. He stated that in

a democratic scheme of things, the military is not supposed to rise above the society from which it springs. But suppose . . . there are maladjust-ments, discontents in the military. If it reaches the point where govern-ment cannot fulfill the needs of the country, should the military rise above society? Should it superimpose itself above society? Should it cor-rect political processes, while remaining in its role? . . . The interaction of the military and political leaders will determine the outcome of the military's role in the future.

When asked what they personally thought, thirteen informants said that they thought that the military should not be involved. One retired colonel said that "their duty is to defend the country, not to indulge in politics." One general said that the military's role "should only be limited to what the constitution and people would want it to play. Otherwise, it could lead to a confusion of its role, it could lead to dictatorship." On the other hand, there were also complaints that the civilians must cooperate to ensure that military personnel do not play political roles. Three informants said that the military had to stay out of politics to ensure that the country did not "become a banana republic," undergoing cycles of democracy and authoritarianism. One informant, a retired navy commander, said that the

media keep saying that the military shouldn't discuss politics. I disagree. The more you discuss, the more the military knows what is its role as a citizen and a soldier. He must realize that these are his constraints—he just cannot be involved in partisan politics. . . . What is the role of the military today? National security. But the meaning of national security is national well-being. So, if you hurt the national well-being, you are a traitor.

Another informant said that the "military should be confined to the military. But in the Third World the military normally takes [a stronger role]. But this role should be turned over, the military should get out."

Two informants said that it depends on conditions in the country. The first informant mentioned NPA growth in power as a reason for why the military should reenter the political sphere. An air force colonel said that if

the country stabilizes, if the government performs well, the military will return to the barracks. They would prefer it. But if the interests of the country are at stake, then the military has no choice. Especially regarding counterinsurgency. A majority in the [Miranda and Ciron] survey agreed that the military should take over if there is a threat of Communist takeover.

Two informants said that they thought that the military should play more of a role. One defended this position by saying that the "AFP is better trained than civilians." Another informant hedged, saying that "there needs to be some kind of participation. But only once the individuals are not connected with the AFP."

Four informants felt a sense of inevitability that the military would become involved in the future, regardless of their personal feelings. They said that such involvement would be due to the insurgency, the government's inability to solve problems, and to the military itself—its sense of frustration that Aquino gave amnesty to the NPA but not to Honasan and the sense that the "system itself does not encourage advice from the military. The military has to find its own power." One retired general said that

our democratic institutions are not well established—they can't work as effective checks and balances to each other. If they did, then the military would have no reason or temptation to intervene in political processes. . . . The military is a corporation like any corporation. Once it takes power, it is hard to relinquish power. The military as a corporation is impatient with democracy. It isn't used to giving reasons for why things are done. . . . If the government succeeds, if there is a change, the military will stay within its prescribed role.

Thus, the military, like the church, found itself still fragmented after the reinstallation of democracy in the Philippines. While the generals wanted to reprofessionalize the institution, to retreat from politics, junior officers did not want to cede their political power. As a result, conflict within the military caused serious political instability as numerous coup attempts were instigated against Aquino's government.

CONCLUSION

The parallel experiences of both the church and the military after 1987 underscore the legacy of authoritarianism. First, both institutions have been permanently politicized and fragmented. The hierarchies of both are incapable of unifying their institutions and reverting back to their traditional, nonpolitical, roles. However, both also have groups within them that continue to operate in the political arena, because their rank and file see political activity as the only way to exert control.

Second, the rank and file in both institutions sense the need to remain in the political arena because there exists a leadership vacuum in the country. Because they fear that the Aquino administration will be ineffectual, they believe that they must remain politically active, to help the Aquino administration govern or to force it to institute reforms. Even members of the two hierarchies accept this argument: they agree that there may exist or arise a situation where Aquino cannot rule on her own and needs their help. Thus, for the sake of stability, even members of the two hierarchies have not ruled out intervention.

It is clear, then, that as a result of both institutions participating in the overthrow of an authoritarian regime and the installation of a democratic government, both reserve the right to reenter the political arena whenever their interests—national or institutional—appear to be threatened. Thus, there is again both an internal reason—institutional fragmentation—and an external reason—a leadership vacuum—for continued political activity on the part of both the church and the military.

III

8 The Philippines in Comparative Perspective

INTRODUCTION

■ As we see from the Philippine case, the experience of authoritarianism changed social institutions such as the church and the military. Both institutions expanded their activities in an attempt to meet the diverging demands of their members. The expansion of their political activity led them to actively oppose the regime, even to the point of forcibly ousting Marcos himself. However, after the installation of democracy, neither the church nor the military returned to their pre–martial law roles. Thus, the effect of authoritarianism lasted after the collapse of the regime.

THE LEGACY OF AUTHORITARIANISM IN THE PHILIPPINES

An authoritarian regime influences the political life of a country not only while it is in power but even after it has been overthrown. By depoliticizing society and personalizing power, an authoritarian leader alters the traditional roles of social institutions such as the church and the military. These institutions were lobbied, both by the leader and by their own members, to take an increasingly active political role. By responding to this pressure, the church and the military found themselves opposing the regime and ousting the leader. As their roles were transformed to encompass more activist participation, it became difficult for the

179

hierarchies of either the church or the military to withdraw from the political arena after the regime ended. Thus, the authoritarian regime inadvertently guaranteed that the institutions would continue to intervene in politics even after the installation of a democratic government.

In part, this process of increased politicization was due to the institutions themselves. New ideologies did indeed emerge in both the church and the military, causing them to rethink their roles. For the church, this new ideology came from the Vatican II reforms, which called upon the church to shift its focus from sacramental duties to the country's political and social conditions. Furthermore, Vatican II and related conferences stressed that the church must not only focus on day-to-day conditions but must engage in social action by sharing the lives of the poor and working for improvement through structural change.

As we saw in chapter 4, the Vatican II reforms transformed the behavior of the church in the Philippines. The traditional role of the church was teaching and sacramental duties. After Vatican II, the church began slowly to move from charity work to social action. For example, in the 1960s, the church sponsored the creation of the Federation of Free Farmers. This shift to political action expanded dramatically in response to the Marcos regime's human rights violations, socioeconomic policies that further eroded the position of the poor, and threats to church officials and doctrine. For example, the church created task forces on human rights and supported a network of Basic Christian Communities. However, this expansion of the church's role was instigated by the lower rank and file of the institution—nuns, priests, and religious brothers—who pressured the church hierarchy to implement reforms and take on an active sociopolitical agenda as espoused by Vatican II.

For the military, the new ideology was a national security doctrine, which encouraged the military to adopt political and socioeconomic tasks to increase the success of its counterinsurgency programs. The military's training was expanded to include such civilian courses as public administration, economic development, and business management. Officers were encouraged to take on traditionally political roles through the creation of civic action programs. Thus, they were directed to undertake public works programs, fill government ministry positions, and manage businesses.

As discussed in chapter 5 the Philippine military's adoption of the national security doctrine changed the way the military acted by expanding its role. The traditional role of the Philippine military was to be professional, following the model of the United States armed forces, on which it was based. The Philippine military adopted the national security doctrine in the 1950s at the behest of the United States, to defeat the Huk rebellion. Its training was expanded and its roles were increased, allowing the military to engage in construction and irrigation projects and rural health care programs. As a result, military officers began to feel equal rather than subservient to politicians and bureaucrats.

The Marcos regime itself also tried to force the institutions to change their behavior in order to increase its own stability. Marcos wanted the church either to support the regime or at least to remain neutral. To gain its support, Marcos tried to cast the options as a government run either by him or by the Communists. Marcos was hoping that this strategy would encourage the church to support him as the lesser of two evils, since the church feared that a Communist government would institute policies counter to its core beliefs. However, as this strategy began to fail, Marcos began to threaten the church as an institution, by threatening to revoke its tax-free status and to pass legislation allowing divorce and birth control, and by harassing and detaining church personnel. In this way, Marcos was hoping that if the church did not openly support the regime, then at least it would remain neutral.

The regime wanted the military not only to be loyal but also to take on roles normally assigned to other branches of government, such as the legislature, the courts, government ministries, and local government. To gain the military's support, the regime greatly expanded the armed forces' size and the salaries of its members. It also promoted and gave privileges to those specific officers who were loyal to Marcos. Those officers who disagreed with the martial law regime or who preferred that the military maintain a professional role found themselves passed over for promotion, reassigned to less desirable duties, or retired. In this way, Marcos hoped to encourage the military as an institution to support him and to discourage any officers considering opposing him, by weeding out those whose loyalties were suspect.

Both the institutions' new ideologies and the regime's attempts to change their behavior caused the church and the military to adopt political roles. Although both the church and the military initially supported the Marcos regime, they eventually withdrew their support and actively worked for its collapse. After 1972, the church initially responded to Marcos's maneuvers by supporting him, even though it was uncomfortable with the idea of an authoritarian regime, because it agreed with Marcos's presentation of choices. However, while the church as an institution was willing to give Marcos the benefit of the doubt, members of the rank and file forced it to slowly take on more political roles and become more critical of the regime. They took a strong oppositionist position, not only because of Vatican II and liberation theology, but also in reaction to the regime's own behavior: its suppression of rights and liberties and its widespread practice of human rights violations, including violations against religious personnel. They called for citizens to boycott elections and for Marcos to end martial law. Furthermore, they identified with the poor and focused on the people's church as a way both to support the call for religious decentralization and to pressure the regime to reform.

Initially, the church hierarchy tried to bridge the widening gap between themselves and the rank and file by issuing pastoral letters that found merit with both sides. Also, the church as an institution began taking a position of "critical collaboration," whereby the church would remain neutral—be neither pro- nor anti-regime—yet would speak out for reform. Third, the church set up the Church-Military Liaison Committee, to try to diminish human rights violation without criticizing the regime in public. However, by the late 1970s, the hierarchy realized that the two positions were ultimately unbridgeable. Thus, they slowly accepted the position of the rank and file as a way of maintaining church unity. To symbolize this shift toward a more activist political role, Cardinal Sin came out in the late 1970s calling for Marcos to step down.

Like the church, the Philippine military initially supported the declaration of martial law. Their expanded roles into domains originally reserved for the judiciary or the bureaucracy fit with their pre–martial law acceptance of the national security doctrine. Furthermore, because Marcos needed the military to support his rule, officers found their positions significantly increased, in terms of pay, privileges, power, and social status. Military officers began to believe that not only were they the equal of politicians and bureaucrats but that now, since their tasks had been expanded into more government sectors, they were superior to them.

However, professionally oriented members of the military began to question the validity of these new political roles. They criticized Marcos's politicization of the military, arguing that the practice of promoting officers based on loyalty rather than ability or years in rank was creating a drop in morale. They also complained that the military was being sidetracked in its primary goal of national security by being asked to take on jobs, such as business management and local government, for which it was neither properly trained nor equipped. Finally, professional members felt humiliated by the fact that the military had been unable to end the rebellion of the Moro National Liberation Front in Mindanao or the guerrilla insurgency fought by the New People's Army. Thus, the military was beginning to view Marcos and his regime as harming rather than helping the military as an institution. This opposition to regime policy began to solidify and expand by the late 1970s, with the emergence of reformist groups within the military, the most notable one being the Reform the Armed Forces of the Philippines Movement.

Growing church and military opposition to Marcos's policies eventually caused both institutions to actively oppose his regime. As discussed in chapter 6 the church openly opposed Marcos's candidacy in the 1986 presidential elections. Before the elections, church leaders drafted a list of possible outcomes and devised what the church's reaction should be to each scenario. They also released pastoral letters warning people to protect the ballot boxes from fraud, allowing people to accept money from candidates but telling them to vote their conscience, and stating that a candidate who wins from cheating must give up his office. Furthermore, the church hierarchy was clearly endorsing the Aquino candidacy, rather than remaining neutral. When Marcos claimed that he had won the election, the church declared that it would not recognize him as the winner. When Enrile and Ramos defected from Marcos and supported Aquino as the rightful winner, the church called on people power to protect them.

By the mid-1980s, disgruntled members of the military had given up on the probability of reforming the regime. Instead, they began to look beyond Marcos. When Marcos was declared the winner of the 1986 election by the National Assembly, RAM supported the church's position that the elections were fraudulent and that people should engage in nonviolent demonstrations to protest the results. Marcos immediately sent orders to have Enrile and Ramos arrested; instead, they resigned their positions in the regime, declared Aquino the rightful winner, and called for Marcos to resign. Over a four-day period, Enrile and Ramos encouraged the military as an institution to withdraw its support from Marcos and to support Aquino.

As a result of the church and the military aggressively acting to oust the regime, Marcos and his entourage fled the country and Aquino gained the presidency. While these institutions were able to successfully replace the regime, this effort did not permanently unify them. Rather, both the church and the military became refragmented after 1986. Hierarchies in both institutions tried to revert to preauthoritarian roles, while rank-and-file members wanted to continue if not expand their political roles. Individual members of the church served in Aquino's cabinet. Moreover, the church as an organization supported her administration in the early years, to lend it stability. For example, the church supported the Constitutional Commission and urged citizens to ratify the new constitution. However, groups within the church began to move in opposite directions soon after Aquino came to power. On the one hand, moderate rightist members of the hierarchy saw Aquino's presidency as an opportunity for the church to revert back to its nonpolitical role, urging the laity to take the lead in politics. They began to purge the institution of suspected leftist personnel as a way to unify the institution and regain control over it. On the other hand, the Left believed that the events of 1986 were merely cosmetic. For the Left, people power and the ensuing collapse of the Marcos regime were merely the beginning of what it believed would be the next, and more significant, struggle, for socioeconomic reform.

When Aquino became president, Enrile became her defense minister and Ramos chief of staff. The military as a whole supported her as well, since both professionalists and RAM members wanted Marcos out. A reform program was begun: to weed out corrupt officers, to make the command structure more professional, to retire overstaying officers and promote junior officers, and to improve counterinsurgency efforts. However, shortly after her inauguration, the military began to take opposite sides. On the one hand, Enrile and RAM members began to have serious disagreements with Aquino. Enrile eventually opposed the new constitution and called into question the legitimacy of Aquino's presidency. RAM felt that Aquino had violated an unwritten agreement made prior to its support of her during the events of 1986, by not giving RAM more power within the cabinet. Officers in general felt that Aquino was taking a position too far to the Left, specifically in negotiating a cease-fire agreement with the New People's Army. Thus, even after the constitution was ratified and the military agreed to abide by it, there were serious doubts about the military's loyalty to the new government. On the other hand, professionalists, who were promoted to the rank of general by Aquino, believed that the institution should be purged of politicos and returned to strict civilian supremacy. A dramatic result of this difference was the fact that from 1986 to 1992, there were seven coup attempts against the Aquino government.

Events in the Philippines support the theory that authoritarian regimes change the roles that social institutions such as the church and the military play in the political arena. Furthermore, this change continues even after the authoritarian regime has collapsed. The discussion below shows that the Philippines is not alone in its experiences with the legacy of authoritarianism.

THE PHILIPPINES IN COMPARATIVE PERSPECTIVE

The Philippines was not the only country to adopt either the Vatican II or the national security ideologies and to be ruled by an authoritarian regime. Indeed, we see that the Philippines' experience is similar to those of other authoritarian countries, such as Argentina, Brazil, and Chile.

The Second Vatican Council and the Church

The Philippines was one of many countries that experienced a change in its church's ideology due to the Vatican II reforms. Indeed, countries in Latin America were particularly targeted for these reforms, since Latin America constituted the largest Catholic area in the Third World. As a result, many Latin American countries not only adopted Vatican II and liberation theology teachings but also pioneered in its further development, both through organized conferences such as Puebla and through the work of individual theologians such as Leonardo Boff (Dodson

1979b; Levine 1981a; Smith 1982; Berryman 1984; Comblin 1984; Boff 1986; Boff and Boff 1986; Berryman 1987; Mainwaring 1986; Pottenger 1989).

The Argentine church adopted a political role early on; over time, however, it shifted its support from the Left to the Right. It initially supported Peron's government, to the point of encouraging its members not to vote for anti-Peronist candidates. By the mid-1950s, the church and state had a falling out, and the church sided with the military (Neuhouser 1989, 241). However, while the church as a whole withdrew, the progressive wing of the church adopted the Vatican II reforms early on, encouraging clergy to become worker-priests—to take menial jobs with the people in order to understand their world (Dodson 1979a, 206; 1979b, 54). For example, clergy belonged to the Movement of Priests for the Third World (MPTW), begun in 1967. This organization attacked the 1966 authoritarian regime within the context of liberation theology and Peronism; through its actions, it eventually was able to convince pastoral-leaning bishops to oppose the regime (Dodson 1979b, 58–59; Deiner 1975). It joined popular efforts, such as "workers' strikes, student demonstrations, barrio protests, and peasant mobilizations" (Dodson 1979b, 58). Furthermore, it sought to actively work for social change, through supporting socialism and the Peronist party (Deiner 1975, 74–76; Dodson 1979a, 217).

The Brazilian church moved more quickly than the Argentinean church and in a more unified fashion, to adopt a progressive role and implement it across the institution's strata (Bruneau 1985). When the National Council of Brazilian Bishops (CNBB) was created in 1952, one of its main goals was social change (Neuhouser 1989, 237). One tactic that the CNBB identified to achieve socioeconomic change was through the creation of BCCs (239). Thus, even before Vatican II, the Brazilian church had begun to organize at the grassroots level, shifting the focus of its work to the everyday lives of the poor. Organizations emerged such as the Catholic Bible Movement, the Christian Family

Movement, Popular Action, and the Movement for Grass-roots Education (Mainwaring 1986). More importantly, this shift was supported by both conservatives and progressives.

In Chile, the church began to move toward implementing a progressive agenda by the late 1950s. Besides Catholic Action programs, the church began land reform and low-income housing projects, tried to make businessmen more aware of the needs of the poor, and supported the Christian Democratic party as a moderate alternative to the Socialists (Smith 1982, 114–15; Sanders 1988, 275; Adriance 1992, 54). As in Argentina, the church in Chile also encouraged clergy to become worker-priests; however, this building of ties with the grassroots was much more successful in Argentina than in Chile (Dodson 1979b, 63). On the other hand, by the late 1960s a group within the church, the Christians for Socialism, took a much more radical position, calling for the church to support the controversial Popular Unity government. The left wing of the church eventually became fragmented, espousing positions to the left of Popular Unity and encouraging the formation of a grassroots church (61–63). Furthermore, by the late 1960s, Chilean bishops began to pull back from the Christian Democratic party and feared the rise of socialism. By 1973, the bishops were considering barring church leaders from membership in Christians for Socialism (Adriance 1992, 58).

The National Security Doctrine and the Military

Countries in Latin America also experienced the emergence of the national security doctrine. In large part, this was due to the United States' encouragement to expand military training to include counterinsurgency methods that would widen the scope of the military (Stepan 1971; Klare and Arnson 1981; Perlmutter 1980a; Khuri 1982; Pion-Berlin 1988; Stepan 1988).

Argentina has had a long history of military intervention in politics. The military instituted coups against the government in 1930, 1943, 1955, 1962, 1966, and 1976 (Rouquie 1987, 272).

This history underscores the fact that the military in Argentina has been autonomous and politicized for most of the twentieth century (Stepan 1988, 114). One result of this repeated intervention was that military officers were used to taking positions on such issues as economic policy and filling roles in ministries and state enterprises (Cavarozzi 1986, 32; Astiz 1969, 872). Consequently, the Argentine military had been fragmented between professionals and politicos even before the 1966 authoritarian regime (Astiz 1969, 865).

Like Argentina's, Brazil's military had a long-standing history of intervening in politics, instituting coups in 1930, 1945, 1954, 1955, and 1964 (Stepan 1977, 58). Brazil is the classic case of a country accepting a national security doctrine, as Stepan used it to test his theory of new professionalism (1971). However, prior to the 1964 coup, the military never remained in office. The experiences of the armed forces during World War II encouraged the military to work for economic modernization, to strengthen the country and raise its position in the world arena (Hayes 1976). As a result, the military shifted its training to stress the interrelationship between economic development and national security. By the early 1960s, Brazilian military officers came to the belief that significant economic and political changes were necessary, that the politicians would not institute these changes, and that they themselves could run the country better because of their new training (Stepan 1977, 57–58).

Of the countries discussed here, the Chilean military was one of the most professional. In particular, it strictly followed civilian supremacy (Arriagada 1991; Rouquie 1987). However, even in the case of Chile, two factors caused the military to take on a more political role by the early 1970s. First, party politics became polarized in the 1960s. In 1964, the Christian Democrats unveiled an aggressive popular platform that changed the rules of the game, allowing new actors, organizations, and issues to emerge. The Right responded by moving farther away from the center and calling for the military to play a less neutral role in politics (Rouquie 1987, 231–32; Arriagada 1991, 82). In 1969, a military regiment revolted, to protect institutional interests. The following year, military officers kidnapped the commander in chief, General René Schneider, to clear the way for a possible coup; the kidnapping ended in Schneider's assassination (Arriagada 1991, 86). Clearly, by 1970, the military's professional traditions had collapsed. This development was hastened by the second factor, which was Allende's own behavior vis-à-vis the military. He offered ministerial positions to military officers, as a way to strengthen his support. However, it had the opposite effect, as military officers were now encouraged to take part in political debates and to form policy on issues outside of military matters (Sigmund 1977). Thus, initial tendencies to take a non-neutral position and to plan a coup against the Socialist government were supported by the officers' experience in day-to-day administration and their realization that Allende was weak.

The Behavior of the Authoritarian Regime

Once in power, the authoritarian regime tries to gain support from the church and the military. This is achieved by linking the rationale for authoritarianism with an institutional interest, such as anticommunism, or by promising to the institutions specific advantages, such as a ban on divorce or increased pay. If these "carrots" fail, then the regime tries to gain cooperation through force, by threatening individuals or whole institutions with sanctions if they do not comply with the regime.

In Argentina, the church initially supported the military coup of 1976. By the mid-1970s, the church had swung away from the progressives and was back under the control of the conservatives. The Movement of Priests for the Third World (MPTW), which began in 1967, ended in 1974. This change was in reaction to leftist terrorism against the 1966 regime and the economic crisis under Isabel Peron's administration. Thus, when the military overthrew Peron in 1976, the church supported the military's actions (Smith 1980, 178–79; Calvert and Calvert 1989, 33).

As in several Latin American countries, the Argentine military formed the regime. For both the 1966 and 1976 coups, the Argentine military was acting out of a sense of new professionalism—that the military had to step in to protect national security by curbing Peronism and instituting sound economic policies (Astiz 1969; Cavarozzi 1986; Pion-Berlin 1988; Smith 1991, 51). The military overthrew Isabel Peron's government in 1976, in reaction to the serious economic crisis that her government had mismanaged (Smith 1991, 230). Again, the military used its national security doctrine as a justification of its actions. It released the Act of National Reorganization, which stated that the military's tasks would include not only the ending of the Montoneros movement but also the implementation of a free market system (Pion-Berlin 1985, 57).

In Brazil, the regime clamped down on all forms of political participation; as a result, the Brazilian church, which had begun speaking out for development before 1964, became subdued. The Right initially supported the regime (Mainwaring 1986, 45–46). In 1970, the National Conference of Bishops tried to take a middle position by criticizing violence regardless of its source, whether sponsored by the regime or by leftist priests. It was not until the mid-1970s that the church returned to its pre-1964 position supporting a progressive stance (Bruneau 1985; Raine 1971).

The Brazilian military overthrew the Goulart government in 1964 and instituted a military regime that focused on economic growth, social harmony, and law and order (Ronning and Keith 1976, 229). To maintain military unity, the junta members were vague about the actual policies they would implement. Furthermore, General Humberto de Alencar Castelo Branco was selected as president in part because it was hoped that he could guarantee military unity behind the regime by spanning the professional and the political camps. Third, junta members suggested that the military would not remain in power indefinitely; to this end, Castelo Branco promised to hold presidential elections in 1965 (Stepan 1971, 216–17). Thus, the military was united in its position of running the regime.

When the military overthrew the Allende government in 1973, the initial response of the Chilean church was muted (Constable and Valenzuela 1991, 29). While it regretted the number of deaths during the overthrow and the early months of the regime, it nevertheless asked the country to cooperate with the military (Smith 1982, 288; Adriance 1992, 58). Behind the scenes, the church tried to convince the regime to end its human rights abuses but was unsuccessful (Sanders 1988, 280). In return for this moderation, the regime allowed the church to continue its work, while the military closed down or censored other institutions (Smith 1982, 289). Thus, the church's behavior was due to a desire "to protect the institutional interests of the Church and from a judgment that the Church could do little except to alleviate some of the effects of repression. It also flowed from the naive trust in promises of the junta and an unwillingness to believe how bad and systematic the brutality actually was" (294).

The Chilean military overthrew the Allende government, claiming that it was protecting the country, and stated that it would remain in power to promote law and order and to dismantle the Socialist political and economic policies of the previous government (Marcella 1979; Arriagada Herrera 1986). The military consolidated its power by creating a junta, ensuring that over 80 percent of the cabinet consisted of military men, and increasing its own budget. Once in office, Pinochet solidified his personal control over the military, and therefore the regime, by purging opponents and elevating himself to the presidency (Remmer 1989, 128–30).

The Church and the Military Join the Opposition

While the church and the military may initially support the authoritarian regime, their loyalty will diminish over time.

Groups within each institution pull away from the leadership's position of supporting the regime and, instead, lobby for the institution to work for political reform. This institutional fragmentation eventually leads the church and the military to join the opposition, as a means of unifying their institutions.

As human rights violations continued under the 1976 regime, and in particular as the military began to target Catholic clergy, the Argentine church slowly began to speak out (Smith 1980, 179–80). However, the clergy did not threaten to break away from the church to form an independent one. As a result, the way in which the clergy worked for socioeconomic reform and political change fragmented the Argentine church less than occurred in other Latin American countries (Dodson 1979b, 60). However, the church, by its quiet reaction, left itself open to the attack from its members that it was being too conciliatory with the regime (Calvert and Calvert 1989, 34).

In Argentina, the economic program instituted by Economy Minister Jose Martinez de Hoz was not uniformly supported by members of the armed forces. Indeed, as the economy declined in early 1980—most dramatically with banks collapsing—the navy publicly stated its disapproval (Pion-Berlin 1985, 61). One result of this fragmentation within the Argentinean military was the 1981 coup, in which President Roberto Viola was overthrown and replaced by another military officer, General Leopoldo Galtieri, who was more of a hard-liner (Zagorski 1988, 421; Smith 1991, 244). When Galtieri led the country into the defeat of the Falklands War, he also was overthrown and replaced by another general, Reynaldo Bignone (Peralta-Ramos 1987, 60).

In Brazil, by the 1970s the church began to speak out against the regime, moving from complaints concerning the economic costs of the regime's development program to protests of human rights abuses and the need for the institution of social democracy (Bruneau 1985, 274–77). The Brazilian church created a Justice and Peace Commission to investigate human rights abuses and work for equitable land distribution; furthermore, it created an extensive BCC network (279–81). The church viewed BCCs as a way to fill the political vacuum created by the regime, particularly at the grassroots level (Krischke 1991, 190).

The Brazilian military began to fragment in reaction to regime performance. Unlike other countries, in Brazil the military's initial reaction was to push the president to institute a more repressive regime. As mass opposition to the regime rose under Castelo Branco, the hard-liners pushed for one of their own, rather than a moderate, to succeed him (Skidmore 1988, 50–51). However, the military remained fragmented under Marshal Artur Costa e Silva, Castelo Branco's successor. Junior officers "complained bitterly that the military *government* was ineffectual and that this reflected badly on the military as an *institution*. They also complained about the decline in the prestige and financial position of the military" (Stepan 1971, 260).

In 1969, Costa e Silva suffered a stroke; in the ensuing battle concerning who would succeed him, the hard-liners were able to veto the vice president as a candidate and replace him with their own candidate (Skidmore 1988). However, the power struggle underscored the fragmentation of the military.

By the second year of the regime, it became harder for the Chilean church to ignore the magnitude of human rights violations being perpetrated by the military. Rank-and-file church members related stories of military abuse of their parishioners and pressed the bishops to openly condemn the regime (Smith 1982, 297; Adriance 1992, 59). By 1974, bishops were divided as to which path the church should take: to cooperate with the regime or to criticize it publicly (Sanders 1988, 281). By 1975, "one-half of the priests and nearly three-fifths of the nuns and laity said that they preferred Church leaders to be more prophetic" (Smith 1982, 304). However, it wasn't until 1976 that the bishops began openly to attack the regime, by releasing a highly critical pastoral letter (307). In 1980, the church decreed that "Catholics who participated in torture were automatically excommunicated" (Sanders 1988, 283). The church offered itself as a base where individuals and organizations could protect themselves from the regime while they worked for its demise (Valenzuela 1984, 71). The main reason for the hierarchy's change of position was that the Christian Democratic party and the church itself were coming under attack from the regime (Smith 1982, 311).

Concerning the military, Pinochet tried to diminish the chances of fragmentation and opposition by weeding out political officers and reinstilling support for old professionalism. However, the economic downturn in 1981 caused the military to fragment into hard-liners and soft-liners, with the former supporting the continuation of Pinochet's personalistic regime and the latter espousing institutionalization to soften the regime's image (Garreton 1986, 103).

Regime Collapse

Eventually, church and military alliances with the opposition cause each institution to work actively to oust the regime. Such behavior ranges from calling for the leaders to voluntarily step down, to actively canvassing votes to overthrow the leader in an election, to threatening to institute a coup against the regime.

The Argentine church's position regarding the 1976 authoritarian regime was more passive than that of churches in other countries. The church hierarchy came out in open support of the regime's nationalist pitch in the Falklands War (Calvert and Calvert 1989, 34). The church did speak out against the regime, through its release of pastoral letters and its work through human rights organizations. Mostly, though, it took a behind-the-scenes approach to try to influence the regime to reform its behavior (Smith 1980, 179–80).

By the early 1980s, the military was severely fragmented, as evidenced by the military overthrowing Viola and Galtieri. By 1983, because of its complete failure—regarding the economy, the Falklands War, and strong government leadership—the junta could not agree on a unified program. Civilians called for the military to cede power. Moderate forces within the military over-ruled the hard-liners and agreed to return power to civilians, even without guarantees of amnesty for human rights violations (Pion-Berlin 1985, 72).

The Brazilian church started working against the military re-gime during the liberalization process, through its vast network of BCCs. From 1974 to 1982, the church significantly increased its efforts at the grassroots level, both in terms of encouraging the spread of BCCs and in stating that their leadership should be mass-based rather than from the institutional church (Mainwar-ing 1986, 178). The church used the popular church as a way to get people to rethink the regime's development programs and to participate in working for an end to the regime. During elections in the early 1980s, the church recommended that people organize their own parties, or support already existing parties, such as the Workers party, in order to replace the military regime with a civilian democratic government (Mainwaring 1986, 231; Della Cava 1989, 156).

By 1978, groups within the military were calling for a return to democracy (Rouquie 1987, 305). Although the opposition's candidate did not win, the new president, General Joao Batista Figueiredo, committed himself to opening up the political arena, with the goal of returning Brazil to democracy. By the 1980s, military officers were calling for redemocratization because of the deteriorating image of the military, due to scandals, human rights violations, and government ineptitude (Skidmore 1988, 272).

By 1980, the Chilean church was calling for the regime to be replaced with a constitutional government. To this end, they supported an open campaign period before the plebiscite on the 1980 constitution (Smith 1982, 310). For the 1988 plebiscite, the "conference of Catholic bishops had pleaded for a consensus candidate, warning that Pinochet's formula could dangerously polarize the nation" (Constable and Valenzuela 1991, 297).

The Chilean military supported Pinochet, for the most part. Although several high-ranking officers did not support Pinochet's candidacy to remain as president, the military in general supported his continuance in office (Valenzuela and Constable 1988, 30; Constable and Valenzuela 1991, 297). However, when Pinochet lost the plebiscite, his military advisors refused Pinochet's request to install emergency powers, stating that "they had all sworn to uphold the constitution" (Constable and Valenzuela 1991, 309). Since Pinochet "had been defeated by his own rules, Chile's military establishment was not prepared to sacrifice honor and unity to salvage his ambitions" (311).

Institutional Activity Under the New Democracies

Once the authoritarian regime exits, the church and the military are faced with an unexpected dilemma. Church and military leadership quickly move to pull their institutions back to preauthoritarian levels of political activity. For example, the church calls for the laity to play a larger role in politics, while the military calls for reform to reprofessionalize the institution. However, groups within each institution will lobby to maintain current levels of political activity. Thus, regime change does not guarantee a return to politics as usual.

In Argentina, the church remained fragmented after the return to democracy in 1983. A significant portion of the bishops still supported the military, because they saw the military as the defender of a Catholic state (Rossing 1986; DeHainaut 1987). On the other hand, they viewed President Raul Alfonsin's administration as harmful, because the president favored a divorce law and the separation of church and state. This split was also evident during the coup attempt while the pope was visiting Argentina for Holy Week. The church hierarchy, unhappy that the pope's visit was being upstaged, sent a cardinal to speak with the rebel leader, who then ended his attempt and went into hiding. Progressive church members, however, supported the people who gathered outside the palace to denounce the coup attempt's threat to democracy (DeHainaut 1987, 582). This institutional fragmentation continued under the Menem administration. At the church's annual meeting, progressive bishops atacked the president for not taking an aggressive approach to end poverty, while more conciliatory bishops spoke in defense of the government, saying that its policies had already improved the conditions of the poor (Church Critical 1991, 965).

Civilian sentiment in Argentina after 1983 centered on reforming the military (Little 1984; Makin 1984). After election to the presidency, Raul Alfonsin tried to diminish the influence of the military by introducing reforms, such as ending the national security doctrine, reorganizing the military, changing its training, cutting its budget, and prosecuting junta members for human rights violations during the Dirty War (Zagorski 1988, 423–24; Pion-Berlin 1991). The military resisted civilian attempts to diminish its power: such resistance ranged from petitioning the government to curtail the prosecution of human rights violations to outright military rebellion (Zagorski 1988). When Carlos Menem became president, the military increased its pressure. In 1989, Menem pardoned two hundred military officers, including Leopoldo Galtieri, found guilty of human rights abuses (200 Military Officers Are Pardoned in Argentina 1989). The following year, military officials publicly stated they feared that the country's economic crisis would threaten democracy but added that they supported Menem (Christian 1990). Military rebels also shifted tactics, from outsider strategies, such as the coup attempt during Holy Week, toward insider strategies, such as supporting Peronist candidates and turning to the mass public to launch a public relations campaign to raise the status of the military. More seriously, however, the rebels also threatened to form a parallel military within the institution (Norden 1990).

In Brazil, the church has continued to take a strong activist position even after the return to democracy. When Jose Sarney assumed the presidency in 1985, relations between his administration and the church were close. Sarney consulted with the bishops on cabinet appointments and specific public policies, to the point where one bishop declared that "the projects of the

Church and the government were very similar" (Bruneau 1988, 295). This close relationship began to deteriorate soon. Sarney fired a church-supported cabinet member, and the minister of justice spoke out against the church as interfering in politics. Sarney visited the Vatican in 1986 and asked the pope to pressure the church to withdraw from politics. In response, several bishops declared that there was little difference between Sarney and the previous authoritarian presidents (296).

The church also took strong positions on specific public policies, especially the design of the Constituent Assembly and an aggressive land reform program (Bruneau 1988, 298). Furthermore, the church tried to go beyond party politics. For the 1989 presidential elections, the church distributed guidelines, discussing specific characteristics rather than specific candidates (Krischke 1991, 187–88). It also turned to the basic communities as an avenue to organize people. In one example, basic communities supported a member for a city council election in 1988. Although the candidate lost, members of the communities said that their experiences in the BCCs made them feel comfortable: "We were afraid of the state. Now we go into politics to struggle for our rights, to talk over priorities about the city with other groups and social classes" (196).

The Brazilian military, under the new democratic government, has been able to hold on to much of its political role. In part, this position of strength is due to the fact that, unlike Argentina's military, it had not lost a war. It is also due to the fact that the man who eventually became president, Jose Sarney, was a longstanding supporter of the military (De Onis 1989, 133). Under Sarney, the military was able to retain control over its organization, including not only promotions but also the position of minister of defense (Stepan 1988, 106; Pion-Berlin 1992, 90–91). The Brazilian military has also played leading roles in nonmilitary issues, including land reform, labor strikes, and international economic relations (Stepan 1988, 108–11). In the 1989 presidential elections, although the military claimed that it did not have veto power, there were questions concerning whether or not it would overthrow the government if Luis Inacio Da Silva (the candidate for the Worker's party) won (De Onis 1989, 136). When Fernando Collor de Mello became president, he tried to curb the military: he cut their budget, refused to raise salaries, replaced military officers in bureaucratic positions with civilians, and ended Sarney's practice of consulting with the military on policy issues (Brooke 1990). When evidence of corruption began to emerge, the military joined politicians in calling for Collor to resign. To underscore their point, the army offered a show of force in Rio and Sao Paulo (1992).

Compared with Argentina and Brazil, the Chilean church has played less of a role in politics since Pinochet stepped down. When Chile returned to democracy in 1990, the church was initially unsure of its role. On the one hand, the new democratic government reinstalled the country's deep-rooted and ideologically diverse party system. However, Pinochet could not be ignored because of his position as commander of the army. Thus, the church felt that its choice was either to play an active role in the new democracy by critiquing it, which could threaten the new government's stability, or to exit from the political arena and give the traditional political actors free rein (Stewart-Gambino 1992b, 41; 1992a, 156). As a result of this dilemma, the church decided to stop being the "voice of the voiceless" and pull out of politics. However, rank-and-file members of the church were pushing the institution to continue its active role. Specifically, they argued that the church must take a leading role in fighting President Patricio Aylwin's contination of Pinochet's economic plan and in publicizing the massive human rights violations committed by the regime (Stewart-Gambino 1992b, 39–40). The president of Chile's bishops' conference took the meeting of the Latin American Congress on Church Social Doctrine, held in Santiago in 1991, as an opportunity to sharply criticize the government, pointing out that the conditions of the poor are the same or worse as under Pinochet's regime (Frasca 1991). The increasing strength of the progressive group can be seen by the election of a progressive candidate for the president of the bishops' conference and the moderate group's distancing itself from the conservatives (Pastor 1992, 7–8).

In contrast to the church, the Chilean military poses the greatest threat to democracy of the three discussed here. The 1980 constitution gave Pinochet, and the military in general, a golden parachute if he lost both the plebiscite and the election. For example, Pinochet and the other military commanders would stay in office until 1997, and he was allowed to appoint nine senators (Constable and Valenzuela 1991, 311). The military has successfully thwarted attempts to press charges concerning human rights violations. A 1978 amnesty law was upheld by the Supreme Court in 1990, thus leaving President Aylwin with the only recourse of holding open hearings without the hope of prosecution (Valenzuela and Constable 1991, 55). To diminish the new government's chances of uncovering military misdeeds, Pinochet incorporated the intelligence branch into the army (56).

CONCLUSION: FRAGILE DEMOCRACIES

This book shows that the installation of an authoritarian regime significantly alters a country's political system, and the effects of these changes are adverse and long-lasting. The regime centralizes power by undermining political institutions. As a result, social institutions are pressured to enter the political arena to represent the interests of their members. When the regime is overthrown, the new democratic government must not only rebuild public trust in political institutions but also contend with the demands of recently activated social institutions.

New democracies in the Philippines, Latin America, and other parts of the Third World face a difficult task in achieving political stability. Authoritarianism changes the roles that institutions play, as well as their relative strengths. These changes increase both the demands placed on the new government and the level of conflict in the system. At the very least, democratic consolidation requires political reform: replacing an authoritarian leader with a democratic one, reintroducing political parties, or drafting new constitutions. However, these reforms by themselves, no matter how well meaning or well thought out, cannot guarantee the success of democracy unless they address the fundamental transformation that the political system has experienced.

Just as these democracies cannot ignore the new political situation, neither can they erase the country's authoritarian experience. New democratic leaders will be unsuccessful if they try to revert to the form of democracy the country had prior to authoritarianism. Groups such as labor unions, which have been frozen out of politics by the authoritarian regime, not only will return to the political arena but also will pressure the new government to address their backlog of demands. The mass public will also have high expectations concerning the new government's performance, while retaining its sense of distrust. During the 1992 presidential elections in the Philippines, for example, mainstream parties and candidates were caught off guard as grassroots organizations started a campaign with the slogan, *No Trapos*—no traditional politicians.

Thus, the most likely result of the experience of authoritarianism is a fragile democracy. The new democratic government will face difficulties in establishing its authority. We have already witnessed coup attempts against the new democracies in the Philippines and Argentina. We have even seen coup attempts in countries that returned to democracy for several years or more and were considered to have successfully consolidated, such as Peru and Venezuela. In the worst case, the new democratic governments will be too fragile to survive. In this scenario, countries may follow the cyclical experiences of Argentina. The legacy of authoritarianism is uncertainty at best and instability at worst.

Appendix
Bibliography
Index

Appendix
Questionnaire for Church and Military Informants

1. Obviously, the church/military played a role in the recent change in government, in 1986.
   a. Was this due to just one or two people in the church/military, or were several groups in the church/military involved?
   b. Can you tell me who some of these people or groups were?

2. When did the church/military become involved in political tasks?
   a. Why?
   b. What did it do?
   c. What effect did this have on the church/military?

3. How did the church's/military's role in politics differ from its role before?

4. Since the events of 1986, has the church/military still been involved in political tasks?
   a. Why?
   b. How?
   c. What effect has this had on the church/military?

5. Do you think the church/military will be more involved or less involved in politics in the future?
   a. Personally, do you think it should play more of a role or less of a role in politics?

6. Can you suggest any church leaders/military officers whom I should also interview?

Bibliography

A Plea From the Pulpit. 1974. *Far Eastern Economic Review* (April 22):22–23.

Abueva, Jose Veloso. 1979. Ideology and Practice in the "New Society." In David A. Rosenberg, ed., *Marcos and Martial Law in the Philippines*. Ithaca: Cornell University Press.

Adriance, Madeleine. 1992. The Paradox of Institutionalization: The Roman Catholic Church in Chile and Brazil. *Sociological Analysis* 53:51–62.

Aguirre, A. P. 1986. *A People's Revolution of Our Time*. Quezon City, Philippines: Pan-Service Master Consultants.

Alves, Maria Helena Moreira. 1988. Dilemmas of the Consolidation of Democracy from the Top in Brazil. *Latin American Perspectives* 15:47–63.

Amnesty International. 1976. *Report of an Amnesty International Mission to the Republic of the Philippines*. London: Amnesty International Publications.

———. 1982. *Report of an Amnesty International Mission to the Republic of the Philippines*. London: Amnesty International Publications.

Anti-Corruption Panel for Philippine Military. 1986. *New York Times*, May 12.

Aquino, Belinda A. 1982. The Philippines Under Marcos. *Current History* 81:160–63.

———. 1986. The Philippines: End of an Era. *Current History* 85:155–58, 184–85.

Arillo, Cecilio T. 1986. *Breakaway*. Manila: Kyodo.

Arriagada Herrera, Genaro. 1986. The Legal and Institutional Framework of the Armed Forces in Chile. In J. Samuel Valenzuela and Arturo Valenzuela, eds., *Military Rule in Chile*. Baltimore: Johns Hopkins University Press.

————. 1991. *Pinochet: The Politics of Power*. Boulder, Colo.: Westview.

Association of Major Religious Superiors of the Philippines (AMRSP). 1986. *AMSRP Mission Statement*. Mimeo.

Astiz, Carlos Alberto. 1969. The Argentine Armed Forces: Their Role and Political Involvement. *Western Political Quarterly* 22:862–78.

Bacalla, Alexander. 1985. I Am Defecting from the AFP to the MFP. Statement at the International Reunion of the Movement for a Free Philippines. Dirksen Senate Office Building, U.S. Senate, Washington, D.C.

Bello, Walden. 1987. *U.S.-Sponsored Low-Intensity Conflict in the Philippines*. San Francisco: Institute for Food and Development Policy.

Bello, Walden, David Kinley, and Elaine Elinson. 1982. Colonization Without an Occupation Force. In Walden Bello, David Kinley, and Elaine Elinson, eds., *Development Debacle: The World Bank in the Philippines*. San Francisco: Institute for Food and Development Policy.

Bello, Walden, David O'Connor, and Robin Broad. 1982. Technocrats Versus Cronies. In Walden Bello, David Kinley, and Elaine Elinson, eds., *Development Debacle: The World Bank in the Philippines*. San Francisco: Institute for Food and Development Policy.

Bernas, Joaquin G. 1988. A PMA Cadet's Anguished Question. *Manila Bulletin*, May 4, 7.

Berryman, Phillip. 1984. *The Religious Roots of Rebellion*. Maryknoll, N.Y.: Orbis.

————. 1986. El Salvador: From Evangelization to Insurrection. In Daniel H. Levine, ed., *Religion and Political Conflict in Latin America*. Chapel Hill: University of North Carolina Press.

————. 1987. *Liberation Theology: Essential Facts About the Revolutionary Movement in Latin America and Beyond*. Philadelphia: Temple University Press.

Boff, Leonardo. 1986. *Church: Charism and Power*. New York: Crossroads.

Boff, Leonardo, and Clodovis Boff. 1986. *Liberation Theology: From Confrontation to Dialogue*. New York: Harper and Row.

Brooke, James. 1990. Brazil's Leader Makes the Army Toe the Line. *New York Times*, September 9.

———. 1992. Brazilian Government Elite Press for President to Resign. *New York Times*, August 29.

Bruneau, Thomas C. 1985. Church and Politics in Brazil: The Genesis of Change. *Journal of Latin American Studies* 17:271–93.

———. 1988. Cooperation or Conflict? The Church in the Brazilian Transition. *Thought* 63:291–307.

Brunello, Anthony R. 1986. Bread and Salvation: The Meaning of Liberation in Liberation Theology. Presented at the annual meeting of the American Political Science Association, Washington, D.C.

Buruma, Ian. 1985. The Church Militant Takes on a New Meaning. *Far Eastern Economic Review* (February 28):77–79.

———. 1986. Bishops in Open Defiance. *Far Eastern Economic Review* (February 27):11–13.

Calvert, Susan, and Peter Calvert. 1989. *Argentina: Political Culture and Instability*. Pittsburgh: University of Pittsburgh Press.

Cardoso, Fernando H. 1986. Entrepreneurs and the Transition Process: The Brazilian Case. In Guillermo O'Donnell, Philippe C. Schmitter, and Laurence Whitehead, eds., *Transitions from Authoritarian Rule*. Vol. 3, Comparative Perspectives. Baltimore: Johns Hopkins University Press.

Carroll, John. 1986a. Some Reflections on Our Philippine Situation Following the Elections. *Pulso* 1:332–35.

———. 1986b. Looking Beyond EDSA (Part I). *Human Society* 42:3–16.

———. 1986c. Looking Beyond EDSA (Part II). *Human Society* 43:1–14.

———. 1988. Report on the Bishops–Businessmen's Survey of Membership Opinion. Quezon City, Philippines: Bishops–Businessmen's Conference.

Catholic Bishops' Conference of the Philippines (CBCP). 1986a. We Must Obey God Rather Than Men. *Pulso* 1:327–31.

———. 1986b. CBCP Pastoral Letter. *Pulso* 1:336–39.

———. 1986c. A Pastoral Letter: On 100 Days of Prayer and Penance. *Pulso* 1:395–97.

Catilo, Aurora C., and Proserpina D. Tapales. 1988. The Legislature.

In Raul P. De Guzman and Mila A. Reforma, eds., *Government and Politics of the Philippines.* Singapore: Oxford University Press.

Cavarozzi, Marcelo. 1986. Political Cycles in Argentina Since 1955. In Guillermo O'Donnell, Philippe C. Schmitter, and Laurence Whitehead, eds., *Transitions from Authoritarian Rule.* Vol. 2, Latin America. Baltimore: Johns Hopkins University Press.

Christian, Shirley. 1990. Price-Shaken Argentina Halts the Money Flow. *New York Times,* January 3.

Church Critical. 1991. *Latin American Monitor* 8:965.

Church Militant. 1979. *The Economist* (October 13):58, 67.

Clad, James. 1986a. Man in the Background. *Far Eastern Economic Review* (July 24):38–39.

———. 1986b. Rumours in a Hothouse. *Far Eastern Economic Review* (November 20):16.

———. 1986c. Marching Orders. *Far Eastern Economic Review* (December 4):10–11.

———. 1987. Military Malcontents. *Far Eastern Economic Review* (September 10):14.

Clad, James, and John Peterman. 1987. Forces for Change. *Far Eastern Economic Review* (November 26):36–37.

Claver, Francisco F. 1986a. The Religious Sector and the New Government. *Pulso* 1:363–73.

———. 1986b. The Church and Revolution: The Philippine Solution. *America.* 356–59.

———. 1986c. The Church and Revolution: The Philippine Solution (Part II). *America.* 376–78.

———. 1987. The Philippine Revolution: A Year Later. *America.* 232–35.

Cohen, Youssef. 1987. Democracy from Above: The Political Origins of Military Dictatorship in Brazil. *World Politics.* 40:30–54.

Comblin, Joseph. 1984. *The Church and the National Security State.* Maryknoll, N.Y.: Orbis.

Constable, Pamela, and Arturo Valenzuela. 1991. *A Nation of Enemies: Chile Under Pinochet.* New York: Norton.

Constantino, Renato. 1988. Civil Liberties and the Aquino Rhetoric. *Midweek,* January 27.

————. 1990. The Cardinal's Sin. Manila, *Daily Globe,* editorial, January 16.

Coronel, Sheila. 1989a. Aquino's Forces Seem to Prevail in Manila Battle. *New York Times,* December 2.

————. 1989b. Philippine Rebels Seize Finance Area and Fight Goes On. *New York Times,* December 3.

Cortes, Irene R. 1980. Executive Legislation: The Philippine Experience. *Philippine Law Journal* 55:1–31.

Das Gupta, Jyotirindra. 1978. A Season of Caesars. *Comparative Politics* 28:315–49.

Davis, Leonard. 1989. *Revolutionary Struggle in the Philippines.* London: Macmillan.

DeHainaut, Raymond K. 1987. Church and Insurrection in Argentina. *The Christian Century* (July 1–8):582–83.

Deiner, John T. 1975. Radicalism in the Argentine Catholic Church. *Government and Opposition* 10:70–89.

Del Carmen, Rolando V. 1979. Constitutionality and Judicial Politics. In David A. Rosenberg, ed., *Marcos and Martial Law in the Philippines.* Ithaca: Cornell University Press.

Della Cava, Ralph. 1989. The "People's Church," The Vatican, and *Abertura.* In Alfred Stepan, ed., *Democratizing Brazil.* New York: Oxford University Press.

De Onis, Juan. 1989. Brazil on the Tightrope Toward Democracy. *Foreign Affairs* 68:127–43.

Diamond, Larry, Juan Linz, and Seymour Martin Lipset, eds. 1989. *Democracy in Developing Countries.* 4 vols. Boulder, Colo.: Lynne Rienner.

Di Palma, Giuseppe. 1990. *To Craft Democracies.* Berkeley: University of California Press.

Dodson, Michael. 1979a. Liberation Theology and Christian Radicalism in Latin America. *Journal of Latin American Studies* 11:203–22.

————. 1979b. The Christian Left in Latin American Politics. *Journal of Interamerican Studies and World Affairs* 21:45–68.

Epstein, Edward C. 1984. Legitimacy, Institutionalization, and Opposition in Exclusionary Bureaucratic-Authoritarian Regimes: The Situation of the 1980's. *Comparative Politics* 17:37–54.

Ermita, Eduardo R. 1987. The New Armed Forces of the Philippines: Problems and Solutions. *Solidarity* 111, March/April: 87–93.

Fabros, Wilfredo. 1988. *The Church and Its Social Involvement in the Philippines, 1930–1972.* Quezon City, Philippines: Ateneo de Manila University Press.

Feldman, David L. 1982. Argentina, 1945–1971: Military Assistance, Military Spending, and the Political Activity of the Armed Forces. *Journal of Interamerican Studies and World Affairs* 24:321–36.

Fenton, James. 1986. The Snap Revolution. *Granta* 18:33–155.

Frasca, Tim. 1991. Church Social Doctrine Debated at Chile Meeting. *National Catholic Reporter,* November 1.

Garreton, Manuel Antonio. 1986. The Political Evolution of the Chilean Military Regime and Problems in the Transition to Democracy. In Guillermo O'Donnell, Philippe C. Schmitter, and Laurence Whitehead, eds., *Transitions from Authoritarian Rule.* Vol. 2, Latin America. Baltimore: Johns Hopkins University Press.

Gastil, Raymond Duncan. 1985. The Past, Present, and Future of Democracy. *Journal of International Affairs* 38:161–79.

General Rejoicing. 1988. *The Economist* (January 30):26.

Giordano, Pasquale T. 1988. *Awakening to Mission: The Philippine Catholic Church 1965–1981.* Quezon City, Philippines: New Day.

Hammond, Paul Y., David J. Louscher, Michael D. Salomone, and Norman A. Graham. 1983. *The Reluctant Supplier: U.S. Decisionmaking for Arms Sales.* Cambridge, Mass.: Oelgeschlager, Gunn, and Hain.

Hardy, Richard P. 1984. *The Philippine Bishops Speak (1968–1983).* Quezon City, Philippines: Maryknoll School of Theology.

Hawes, Gary. 1987. *The Philippine State and the Marcos Regime: The Politics of Export.* Ithaca: Cornell University Press.

Hayes, Robert A. 1976. The Military Club and National Politics in Brazil. In Henry H. Keith and Robert A. Hayes, eds., *Perspectives on Armed Politics in Brazil.* Tempe: Center for Latin American Studies, Arizona State University.

Hernandez, Carolina G. 1979. The Extent of Civilian Control of the Military in the Philippines, 1946–1976. Ph.D. dissertation, State University of New York at Buffalo.

———. 1985a. Constitutional Authoritarianism and the Prospects of Democracy in the Philippines. *Journal of International Affairs* 38:243–58.

———. 1985b. The Philippines. In Zakaria Haji Ahmad and Harold Crouch, eds., *Military-Civilian Relations in South-East Asia.* New York: Oxford University Press.

———. 1987. The Philippine Military in the 21st Century. In F. Sionil Jose, ed., *A Filipino Agenda for the 21st Century.* Manila: Solidaridad.

———. 1988. The Philippines in 1987: Challenges of Redemocratization. *Asian Survey* 28:229–41.

Higley, John, and Richard Gunther, eds. 1992. *Elites and Democratic Consolidation in Latin America and Southern Europe.* Cambridge: Cambridge University Press.

Hirschman, Albert O. 1970. *Exit, Voice, and Loyalty: Responses to Declines in Firms, Organizations, and States.* Cambridge: Harvard University Press.

Huntington, Samuel P. 1968. *Political Order in Changing Societies.* New Haven: Yale University Press.

———. 1984. Will More Countries Become Democratic? *Political Science Quarterly* 99:193–218.

———. 1991. *The Third Wave: Democratization in the Late Twentieth Century.* Norman: University of Oklahoma Press.

Hyman, Elizabeth. 1972. Soldiers in Politics: New Insights on Latin American Armed Forces. *Political Science Quarterly* 87:401–18.

I Am Afraid of the Future. 1976. *Far Eastern Economic Review* (December 10):10–12.

Institute on Church and Social Issues (ICSI) Staff. 1986. Post-Election Scenarios. *Pulso* 1:311–26.

Janowitz, Morris. 1964. *The Military in the Political Development of New Nations.* Chicago: University of Chicago Press.

Jenkins, David. 1983a. All the President's Men. *Far Eastern Economic Review* (March 10):15–16.

———. 1983b. The Generals Watch the Favourites in the Succession Stakes. *Far Eastern Economic Review* (March 10):20–21.

Joannes Paulus II. 1986. Letter of His Holiness Pope John Paul II to the Bishops of the Philippines. *Pulso* 1:391–94.

Johnson, Bryan. 1987. *The Four Days of Courage.* New York: Free Press.

Karl, Terry Lynn. 1990. Dilemmas of Democratization in Latin America. *Comparative Politics* 23:1–22.

Kessler, Richard J. 1989. *Rebellion and Repression in the Philippines.* New Haven: Yale University Press.

Khuri, Fuad I. 1982. The Study of Civil-Military Relations in Modernizing Societies in the Middle East: A Critical Assessment. In Roman Kolkowicz and Andrzej Korbonski, eds., *Soldiers, Peasants, and Bureaucrats.* London: Allen and Unwin.

Klare, Michael T., and Cynthia Arnson. 1981. *Supplying Repression: U.S. Support for Authoritarian Regimes Abroad.* Washington, D.C.: Institute for Policy Studies.

Kossok, Manfred. 1972. The Armed Forces in Latin America: Potential for Changes in Political and Social Functions. *Journal of Interamerican Studies and World Affairs* 14:375–98.

Krasner, Stephen D. 1984. Approaches to the State: Conceptions and Historical Dynamics. *Comparative Politics* 16:223–46.

Krischke, Paulo J. 1991. Church Base Communities and Democratic Change in Brazilian Society. *Comparative Political Studies* 24:186–210.

Lande, Carl H. 1986. The Political Crisis. In John Bresnan, ed., *Crisis in the Philippines: The Marcos Era and Beyond.* Princeton: Princeton University Press.

Lande, Carl H., and Richard Hooley. 1986. Aquino Takes Charge. *Foreign Affairs* 64:1087–1107.

The Laurel Report on the August 28 Mutiny. 1987. *Manila Standard,* September 19.

Leftward Christian Soldiers? 1982. *The Economist* (December 4): 100.

Levine, Daniel H. 1978. Venezuela Since 1958: The Consolidation of Democratic Politics. In Juan Linz and Alfred Stepan, eds., *The Breakdown of Democratic Regimes: Latin America.* Baltimore: Johns Hopkins University Press.

————. 1981a. *Religion and Politics in Latin America: The Catholic Church in Venezuela and Colombia.* Princeton: Princeton University Press.

————. 1981b. Religion, Society, and Politics: States of the Art. *Latin American Research Review* 16:185–209.

————. 1984. Religion and Politics: Dimensions of Renewal. *Thought* 59:117–35.

————. 1985. Religion and Politics: Drawing Lines, Understanding Change. *Latin American Research Review* 20:185–201.

————. 1986. Colombia: The Institutional Church and the Popular. In Daniel H. Levine, ed., *Religion and Political Conflict in Latin America.* Chapel Hill: University of North Carolina Press.

Levine, Daniel H., and Scott Mainwaring. 1989. Religion and Popular Protest in Latin America: Contrasting Experiences. In Susan Eckstein, ed., *Power and Popular Protest: Latin American Social Movements.* Berkeley: University of California Press.

Lieuwen, Edwin. 1960. *Arms and Politics in Latin America.* New York: Praeger.

————. 1962. Militarism and Politics in Latin America. In John J. Johnson, ed., *The Role of the Military in Underdeveloped Countries.* Princeton: Princeton University Press.

Linz, Juan J. 1964. An Authoritarian Regime: Spain. In Erik Allardt and Yrjo Littunen, eds., *Cleavages, Ideologies, Party Systems.* Helsinki: Academic Bookstore.

————. 1973. Opposition to and Under an Authoritarian Regime: The Case of Spain. In Robert A. Dahl, ed., *Regimes and Oppositions.* New Haven: Yale University Press.

Little, Walter. 1984. Civil-Military Relations in Contemporary Argentina. *Government and Opposition* 19:207–24.

Lopez, George A., and Michael Stohl, eds. 1987. *Liberalization and Redemocratization in Latin America.* Westport, Conn.: Greenwood.

McBeth, John. 1989. Division of Loyalties. *Far Eastern Economic Review* (December 28):19.

McCann, Frank D., Jr. 1979. Origins of the "New Professionalism" of the Brazilian Army. *Journal of Interamerican Studies and World Affairs* 21:505–22.

—————. 1980. The Brazilian Army and the Problem of Mission, 1939–1964. *Journal of Latin American Studies* 12:107–26.

McClintock, Cynthia. 1989. The Prospects for Democratic Consolidation in a "Least Likely" Case: Peru. *Comparative Politics* 21:127–48.

McCoy, Alfred W. 1990. RAM Boys Series. *Philippine Daily Inquirer,* February.

Machado, Kit G. 1979. The Philippines in 1978: Authoritarian Consolidation Continues. *Asian Survey* 19:131–40.

Mainwaring, Scott. 1986. *The Catholic Church and Politics in Brazil, 1916–1985.* Stanford: Stanford University Press.

—————. 1988. Political Parties and Democratization in Brazil and the Southern Cone. *Comparative Politics* 21:91–120.

—————. 1989. Grass-roots Catholic Groups and Politics in Brazil. In Scott Mainwaring and Alexander Wilde, eds., *The Progressive Church in Latin America.* Notre Dame, Ind.: University of Notre Dame Press.

Makin, Guillermo. 1984. The Argentine Process of Demilitarization: 1980–1983. *Government and Opposition* 19:225–38.

Malin, Herbert S. 1985. The Philippines in 1984: Grappling with Crisis. *Asian Survey* 25:198–205.

Manila Describes Evidence on Plot. 1989. *New York Times,* December 29.

Marcella, Gabriel. 1979. The Chilean Military Government and the Prospects for Transition to Democracy. *Inter-American Economic Affairs* 33:3–19.

March, James G., and Johan P. Olsen. 1984. The New Institutionalism: Organizational Factors in Political Life. *American Political Science Review* 78:734–49.

Marcos: The Safety Catch Is Released. 1975. *Far Eastern Economic Review,* (February 14):12.

Miranda, Felipe B., and Ruben F. Ciron. 1988. Development and the Military in the Philippines: Military Perceptions in a Time of Continuing Crisis. Occasional paper. Social Weather Stations, Quezon City, Philippines.

Mydans, Seth. 1985. Marcos Declares He'll Call a Vote Early Next Year. *New York Times,* November 4.

———. 1986. Manila Defense Chief Sees Discipline Tightening. *New York Times*, December 13.

———. 1988a. A Stern Manila Hunts Mutineer, Again. *New York Times*, April 3.

———. 1988b. Filipino Army Awaits Move By Mutineer. New York Times, April 10.

Needler, Martin C. 1975. Military Motivations in the Seizure of Power. *Latin American Research Review* 10:63–80.

Neher, Clark D. 1981. The Philippines in 1980: The Gathering Storm. *Asian Survey* 21:261–73.

Nemenzo, Francisco. 1987. A Season of Coups (Reflections on the Military in Politics). *Kasarinlan* 2:5–14.

Neuhouser, Kevin. 1989. The Radicalization of the Brazilian Catholic Church in Comparative Perspective. *American Sociological Review* 54:233–44.

Noble, Lela Garner. 1986. Politics in the Marcos Era. In John Bresnan, ed., *Crisis in the Philippines*. Princeton: Princeton University Press.

Norden, Deborah L. 1990. Rebels with a Cause: The Argentine Carapintadas. Paper prepared for the 1990 Midwest Political Science Annual Meeting, Chicago.

North, Liisa, and Jose Nun. 1978. A Military Coup Is a Military Coup . . . Or Is It? *Canadian Journal of Political Science* 11:165–74.

Nunn, Frederick M. 1975. New Thoughts on Military Intervention in Latin American Politics: The Chilean Case. *Journal of Latin American Studies* 7:271–304.

Ocampo, Sheilah. 1978a. Crisis in the Cloisters. *Far Eastern Economic Review* (September 1):24.

———. 1978b. A New Role for the Forces. *Far Eastern Economic Review* (October 13):37–38.

———. 1978c. A Big Family Argument. *Far Eastern Economic Review* (November 24):17–18.

———. 1979. Seeking Integrity for Stability. *Far Eastern Economic Review* (April 27):32–34.

———. 1981a. A Pope Among the Politicos. *Far Eastern Economic Review* (February 13):16–17.

————. 1981b. Marcos Cuts the Knot. *Far Eastern Economic Review* (August 7):12.

————. 1982a. Pushed Into Purgatory. *Far Eastern Economic Review* (September 10):31–32.

————. 1982b. The Gun and the Crucifix. *Far Eastern Economic Review* (December 10):38–39.

Ocampo-Kalfors, Sheilah. 1983. More Sinned Against . . . . *Far Eastern Economic Review* (February 10):10–11.

O'Donnell, Guillermo A. 1978. Reflections on the Patterns of Change in the Bureaucratic-Authoritarian State. *Latin American Research Review* 13:3–38.

————. 1979. *Modernization and Bureaucratic-Authoritarianism: Studies in South American Politics*. Berkeley: Institute of International Studies, University of California.

O'Donnell, Guillermo. Philippe C. Schmitter, and Laurence Whitehead, eds. 1986. *Transitions from Authoritarian Rule*. 4 vols. Baltimore: Johns Hopkins University Press.

Overholt, William H. 1986. The Rise and Fall of Ferdinand Marcos. *Asian Survey* 26:1137–63.

Pastor, Anibal. 1992. Golpe al Timon. *Pastoral Popular* 224–225:7–8.

Pear, Robert. 1989. Philippine Rebels Remain at Large. *New York Times*, December 14.

Peralta-Ramos, Monica. 1987. Toward an Analysis of the Structural Basis of Coercion in Argentina: The Behavior of the Major Fractions of the Bourgeoisie, 1976–1983. In Monica Peralta-Ramos and Carlos H. Waisman, eds., *From Military Rule to Liberal Democracy in Argentina*. Boulder, Colo.: Westview.

Perlmutter, Amos. 1980a. *Political Roles and Military Rulers*. London: Cass.

————. 1980b. The Comparative Analysis of Military Regimes: Formations, Aspirations, and Achievements. *World Politics* 33:96–120.

————. 1982. Civil-Military Relations in Socialist Authoritarian and Praetorian States: Prospects and Retrospects. In Roman Kolkowicz and Andrzej Karbonski, eds., *Soldiers, Peasants, and Bureaucrats*. London: Allen and Unwin.

Pimentel, Benjamin. 1987. What's Happening to Our Country, General? *Midweek,* December 16.

Pion-Berlin, David. 1985. The Fall of Military Rule in Argentina: 1976–1983. *Journal of Interamerican Studies and World Affairs* 27:55–76.

———. 1988. The National Security Doctrine, Military Threat Perception, and the "Dirty War" in Argentina. *Comparative Political Studies* 21:382–407.

———. 1991. Between Confrontation and Accommodation: Military and Government Policy in Democratic Argentina. *Journal of Latin American Studies* 23:543–71.

———. 1992. Military Autonomy and Emerging Democracies in South America. *Comparative Politics* 25:83–102.

Pottenger, John R. 1989. *The Political Theory of Liberation Theology.* Albany: State University of New York Press.

Przeworski, Adam. 1986. Some Problems in the Study of the Transition to Democracy. In Guillermo O'Donnell, Philippe C. Schmitter, and Laurence Whitehead, eds., *Transitions from Authoritarian Rule.* Vol. 3, Comparative Perspectives. Baltimore: Johns Hopkins University Press.

———. 1991. *Democracy and the Market.* Cambridge: Cambridge University Press.

Raine, Philip. 1971. The Catholic Church in Brazil. *Journal of Interamerican Studies and World Affairs* 13:279–95.

RAM to Remain After Undergoing "Redirection." 1986. *Ang Pahayagang Malaya,* November 29.

Ramos, Fidel V. 1987. Feedback: Letter from General Fidel Ramos. *Solidarity* 111 (March/April): 85–86.

Remmer, Karen, 1985. Redemocratization and the Impact of Authoritarian Rule in Latin America. *Comparative Politics* 17:253–75.

———. 1989. *Military Rule in Latin America.* Boston: Unwin Hyman.

———. 1991. New Wine or Old Bottlenecks? *Comparative Politics* 23:479–95.

Rochon, Thomas R., and Michael J. Mitchell. 1989. Social Bases of the Transition to Democracy in Brazil. *Comparative Politics* 21:307–22.

Ronning, C. Neale, and Henry H. Keith. 1976. Shrinking the Political Arena: Military Government in Brazil Since 1964. In Henry H. Keith and Robert A. Hayes, eds., *Perspectives on Armed Politics in Brazil.* Tempe: Center for Latin American Studies, Arizona State University.

Rosenberg, David A. 1979. Introduction: Creating a "New Society." In David A. Rosenberg, ed., *Marcos and Martial Law in the Philippines.* Ithaca: Cornell University Press.

Rossing, Barbara R. 1986. Democratic Argentina. *Christianity and Crisis* (May 5):149–51.

Rouquie, Alain. 1987. *The Military and the State in Latin America.* Berkeley: University of California Press.

Rustow, Dankwart A. 1970. Transitions to Democracy. *Comparative Politics* 2:337–63.

Sacerdoti, Guy. 1983. Pressure from the Pulpit. *Far Eastern Economic Review* (September 22):18–20.

———. 1984a. A Test for the System. *Far Eastern Economic Review* (November 8):14–15.

———. 1984b. Military in the Wings. *Far Eastern Economic Review* (December 6):15–17.

———. 1985a. Not Guilty—52 Times. *Far Eastern Economic Review* (February 14):16.

———. 1985b. Fighting the Rebels with Slide Shows and Guns. *Far Eastern Economic Review* (November 21):58–59.

———. 1986a. A Question of Fairness. *Far Eastern Economic Review* (January 30):11–12.

———. 1986b. The Comelec Factor. *Far Eastern Economic Review* (February 13):13–15.

———. 1986c. March Towards Reform. *Far Eastern Economic Review* (May 29) 132:40–43.

———. 1986d. Shadow of the Past. *Far Eastern Economic Review* (May 29):42–43.

Sacerdoti, Guy, and Rodney Tasker. 1983. The Military Card in Play. *Far Eastern Economic Review* (October 13):15–17.

Saints and Sinners. 1981. *The Economist* (February 14):99.

Sanders, Thomas G. 1988. Catholicism and Democracy: The Case of Chile. *Thought* 63:272–90.

Sanger, David E. 1989a. Reliving the Rebellion, Diplomat Speaks Softly. *New York Times* (December 19):19.

―――. 1989b. In Manila Coup Effort, Economy Is Big Victim. *New York Times,* December 20.

Scott, James C. 1985. *Weapons of the Weak: Everyday Forms of Peasant Resistance.* New Haven: Yale University Press.

Seligson, Mitchell A. 1987. Democratization in Latin America: The Current Cycle. In James M. Malloy and Mitchell A. Seligson, eds., *Authoritarians and Democrats: Regime Transition in Latin America.* Pittsburgh: University of Pittsburgh Press.

Selochan, Viberto. 1988. *Could the Military Govern the Philippines?* Working Paper #160. Canberra: Strategic and Defense Studies Centre, Research School of Pacific Studies, Australia National University.

Shaplen, Robert. 1986a. A Reporter at Large: From Marcos to Aquino, Part I. *New Yorker* (August 25).

―――. 1986b. A Reporter at Large: From Marcos to Aquino, Part II. *New Yorker* (September 1).

Shoesmith, Dennis. 1985. The Church. In R. J. May and Francisco Nemenzo, Jr., eds., *The Philippines After Marcos.* London: Croom Helm.

Sigmund, Paul E. 1977. *The Overthrow of Allende and the Politics of Chile, 1964–1976.* Pittsburgh: University of Pittsburgh Press.

Sin, Cardinal Jaime L. 1988. Infiltration and the Church. *Wall Street Journal,* March 14.

Skidmore, Thomas E. 1988. *The Politics of Military Rule in Brazil, 1964–85.* New York: Oxford University Press.

Smith, Brian. 1975. Religion and Social Change: Classical Theories and New Formulations in the Context of Recent Developments in Latin America. *Latin American Research Review* 10:3–34.

―――. 1980. Churches and Human Rights in Latin America: Recent Trends on the Subcontinent. In Daniel H. Levine, ed., *Churches and Politics in Latin America.* Beverly Hills: Sage.

―――. 1982. *The Church and Politics in Chile: Challenges to Modern Catholicism.* Princeton: Princeton University Press.

―――. 1986. Old Allies, New Enemies: The Catholic Church as Opposition to Military Rule in Chile, 1973–1979. In J. Samuel

Valenzuela and Arturo Valenzuela, eds., *Military Rule in Chile: Dictatorship and Oppositions.* Baltimore: Johns Hopkins University Press.

Smith, William C. 1991. *Authoritarianism and the Crisis of the Argentine Political Economy.* Stanford: Stanford University Press.

Social Weather Stations. 1988. Public Opinion on the Honasan Escape. Social Weather Bulletin Series 1988, No. 5. Quezon City, Philippines.

Stauffer, Robert B. 1977. Philippine Corporatism: A Note on the "New Society." *Asian Survey* 17:393–407.

———. 1979. The Political Economy of Refeudalization. In David A. Rosenberg, ed., *Marcos and Martial Law in the Philippines.* Ithaca: Cornell University Press.

Stepan, Alfred. 1971. *The Military in Politics: Changing Patterns in Brazil.* Princeton: Princeton University Press.

———. 1977. The New Professionalism of Internal Warfare and Military Role Expansion. In Stepan, ed., *Authoritarian Brazil: Origins, Policies, and Future.* New Haven: Yale University Press.

———. 1978. *The State and Society: Peru in Comparative Perspective.* Princeton: Princeton University Press.

———. 1986. Paths Toward Redemocratization: Theoretical and Comparative Considerations. In Guillermo O'Donnell, Philippe C. Schmitter, and Laurence Whitehead, eds., *Transitions from Authoritarian Rule.* Vol. 3, Comparative Politics. Baltimore: Johns Hopkins University Press.

———. 1988. *Rethinking Military Politics: Brazil and the Southern Cone.* Princeton: Princeton University Press.

Stewart-Gambino, Hannah W. 1992a. *The Church and Politics in the Chilean Countryside.* Boulder, Colo.: Westview.

———. 1992b. Refining the Changes and Politics in Chile. In Edward L. Cleary and Hannah Stewart-Gambino, eds., *Conflict and Competition: The Latin American Church in a Changing Environment.* Boulder, Colo.: Lynne Rienner.

Stockwin, Harvey. 1974a. We Cannot Jail a Man Indefinitely and Still Call Ourselves Christian. *Far Eastern Economic Review* (December 6):16–18.

———. 1974b. A Placating Gesture to the Church. *Far Eastern Economic Review* (December 13):14.

Tancangco, Luzviminda G. 1988. The Electoral System and Political Parties in the Philippines. In Raul P. De Guzman and Mila A. Reforma, eds., *Government and Politics of the Philippines.* Singapore: Oxford University Press.

Tasker, Rodney. 1976a. Marcos Flays Pulpit Politica. *Far Eastern Economic Review* (December 10):10–12.

———. 1976b. Another Censure for the Church. *Far Eastern Economic Review* (December 17):14–15.

———. 1977. Church Forms a United Front. *Far Eastern Economic Review* (February 25):20–22.

———. 1984a. Faction Stations. *Far Eastern Economic Review* (March 8):38–39.

———. 1984b. Rivalry in the Ranks. *Far Eastern Economic Review* (March 8):39–40.

———. 1985. The Hidden Hand. *Far Eastern Economic Review* (August 1):10–11.

———. 1986a. Arms and the Men. *Far Eastern Economic Review* (February 6):25–27.

———. 1986b. Ver Still There, But RAM Has to Be Reckoned With. *Far Eastern Economic Review* (February 27):14–15.

———. 1986c. Re-form and Reform. *Far Eastern Economic Review* (March 13):14–15.

———. 1986d. A Soldier's Soldier Enters the Political Theatre. *Far Eastern Economic Review* (December 4):21.

———. 1986e. A Delicate Balance. *Far Eastern Economic Review* (December 11):50–51.

———. 1987. The Religion Factor. *Far Eastern Economic Review* (January 15):16–17.

Tasker, Rodney, and Sheilah Ocampo. 1981. In the Pope's Shadow. *Far Eastern Economic Review* (February 27):8–10.

Timberman, David G. 1990. The Philippines in 1989: A Good Year Turns Sour. *Asian Survey* 30:167–77.

200 Military Officers Are Pardoned in Argentina. 1989. *New York Times,* October 8.

Valenzuela, Arturo. 1984. Chile's Political Instability. *Current History* 83:68–72, 88–89.

Valenzuela, Arturo, and Pamela Constable. 1988. Plebiscite in Chile: End of the Pinochet Era? *Current History* 87:29–33, 41.

————. 1991. Democracy in Chile. *Current History* 90:53–56, 84–85.

Vallier, Ivan. 1967. Religious Elites: Differentiations and Developments in Roman Catholicism. In Seymour Martin Lipset and Aldo Solari, eds., *Elites in Latin America*. New York: Oxford University Press.

————. 1970. *Catholicism, Social Control, and Modernization in Latin America*. Englewood Cliffs, N.J.: Prentice-Hall.

Villegas, Bernardo M. 1987. The Philippines in 1986: Democratic Reconstruction in the Post-Marcos Era. *Asian Survey* 27:194–205.

Viola, Eduardo, and Scott Mainwaring. 1985. Transitions to Democracy: Brazil and Argentina in the 1980s. *Journal of International Affairs* 38:193–219.

Vokey, Richard. 1979. With the Pope on Their Side. *Far Eastern Economic Review* (July 20):28–30.

————. 1981. Anxiety Over the Army's Role. *Far Eastern Economic Review* (February 5):28–31.

Walsh, Mary Williams. 1988. Mixed Loyalties: Military Academy Rife with Discontent, Reflecting the Army's Politicization. *Asian Wall Street Journal Weekly,* October 10.

Wesson, Robert, and David V. Fleischer. 1983. *Brazil in Transition*. New York: Praeger.

Wideman, Bernard. 1976. The Christian "Party." *Far Eastern Economic Review* (March 5):26–27.

Wise, William M. 1987. The Philippine Military After Marcos. In Carl H. Lande, ed., *Rebuilding a Nation: Philippine Challenges and American Policy*. Washington, D.C.: Washington Institute for Values in Public Policy.

The Wrath of Cardinal Sin. 1978. *Far Eastern Economic Review* (June 2):35–36.

Wurfel, David. 1977. Martial Law in the Philippines: The Methods of Regime Survival. *Pacific Affairs* 50:5–30.

————. 1988. *Filipino Politics: Development and Decay*. Ithaca: Cornell University Press.

Youngblood, Robert L. 1978. Church Opposition to Martial Law in the Philippines. *Asian Survey* 18:505–20.

————. 1982. Structural Imperialism: An Analysis of the Catholic Bishops' Conference of the Philippines. *Comparative Political Studies* 15:29–56.

———. 1987a. Church and State in the Philippines: Some Implications for United States Policy. In Carl H. Lande, ed., *Rebuilding a Nation: Philippine Challenges and American Policy.* Washington, D.C.: Washington Institute for Values in Public Policy.

———. 1987b. The Corazon Aquino "Miracle" and the Philippine Churches. *Asian Survey* 27:1240–55.

———. 1989. Aquino and the Churches: A "Constructive Critical Solidarity." Presented at the annual meeting of the Association of Asian Studies, Washington, D.C.

———. 1990. *Marcos Against the Church.* Ithaca: Cornell University Press.

Zagorski, Paul W. 1988. Civil-Military Relations and Argentine Democracy. *Armed Forces and Society* 14:407–32.

Index